World Famous SPIES & SPYMASTERS

Vikas Khatri

PUSTAK MAHAL®

Publishers
Pustak Mahal®

J-3/16 , Daryaganj, New Delhi-110002
☎ 23276539, 23272783, 23272784 • *Fax:* 011-23260518
E-mail: info@pustakmahal.com • *Website:* www.pustakmahal.com

Sales Centre

- 10-B, Netaji Subhash Marg, Daryaganj, New Delhi-110002
  ☎ 23268292, 23268293, 23279900 • *Fax:* 011-23280567
  E-mail: rapidexdelhi@indiatimes.com
- **Hind Pustak Bhawan**
  6686, Khari Baoli, Delhi-110006
  ☎ 23944314, 23911979

Branches

Bengaluru: ☎ 080-22234025 • *Telefax:* 080-22240209
E-mail: pustak@airtelmail.in • pustak@sancharnet.in
Mumbai: ☎ 022-22010941, 022-22053387
E-mail: rapidex@bom5.vsnl.net.in
Patna: ☎ 0612-3294193 • *Telefax:* 0612-2302719
E-mail: rapidexptn@rediffmail.com
Hyderabad: *Telefax:* 040-24737290
E-mail: pustakmahalhyd@yahoo.co.in

ISBN 978-81-223-1209-6

Edition: 2011

Printed at : Param Offsetters, Okhla, New Delhi-110020

Contents

❖❖❖

Introduction

Espionage is the practice of spying to acquire information. It involves gaining access to the desired information, actually acquiring the information, and then conveying it to an intelligence agency for evaluation. Although espionage is only one aspect of intelligence operations, it is an important source of information for any government attempting to learn the secrets of other nations. Industries also use it to gain the fruits of another firm's research without performing the labour, and political factions use it hoping to preempt and undermine their rivals.

Methods

Espionage is chosen over other means of intelligence collection when physical acquisition of a document or object is required, or when only an on-the-spot observer can procure the information desired. Espionage methods are generally the same whether conducted for reasons of national security, economic gain, or political leverage. Agents can install wiretaps or "bugs" (concealed microphones), steal, buy, or transcribe documents, steal equipment, or simply observe with their own eyes. Agents convey the information thus acquired to a parent intelligence service by radio, by leaving the information at a "drop", or by hand delivery either in person or through a courier.

There are several different types of espionage agents. The professional spy popularised in fiction is often an "illegal" who passes him – or herself off as a fictitious person complete with forged identity papers. The "illegal" may work alone or establish a spy ring. Another type of agent is the part-time spy who maintains an open, legal existence (often as a diplomat or businessperson) and conducts espionage on the side. A "plant" is an agent who is positioned within the target organisation for an extended period of time. The "insider" or "recruit" is a member of the target organisation who has shifted loyalties and who procures and provides information on a regular basis. Historically, the "insider" is probably the most productive type of agent. "Insiders" can be recruited by ideological appeals, by offers of money, or by blackmail.

Counterespionage

Counterespionage, which is the prevention and thwarting of hostile espionage, utilises some of the same methods as espionage itself. The best method of crippling an adversary's espionage program is by planting one's own agent (a "mole") into the hostile espionage organisation. Another successful practice is to capture hostile spies and turn them into "double agents" who channel false information to their original employers. Counterespionage frequently crosses over into law enforcement, for many espionage activities violate domestic laws. Criminal prosecution is often an effective means of neutralising a hostile spy. Hence the Federal Bureau of Investigation (FBI), a law enforcement agency, is also responsible for counterespionage in the United States.

History

Espionage has been practiced throughout history. The Old Testament reports that both Moses and Joshua employed spies. The Chinese philosopher Sun Zi (Sun Tzu) wrote knowingly of spies around 400 BC. Modern espionage had its origins with Sir Francis Walsingham, the spymaster for Queen Elizabeth I of England, whose agents infiltrated the courts of Europe. The Frenchman Joseph Fouche was a master of counterespionage whose secret police supported the regime of Napoleon Bonaparte. The spies who appear in early American history, such as Nathan Hale in the American Revolution, as well as Belle Boyd and Elizabeth Van Lew in the Civil War, were generally amateur volunteers.

Espionage had little impact on policy or strategy in World War I. During World War II, however, some very impressive feats of espionage took place. Soviet espionage groups such as the Rote Kapelle ("Red Orchestra") and the Richard Sorge ring penetrated the German and Japanese high commands, respectively. On the other hand, German attempts to infiltrate Britain backfired when British counterespionage made double agents out of 40 German spies (the "Double Cross" operation).

The cold war brought the United States fully into the world of espionage. Although it has proved very difficult to introduce spies into certain closed societies. Defectors and "insiders" have, from time to time, conducted valuable espionage on behalf of the Western powers. After its division into east and west, Germany became a focal point of cold war espionage. The cultural homogeneity of the two Germanys facilitated infiltration. The division of families and friends by the Iron Curtain frequently meant that spies could find hospitable contacts. It also raised opportunities for recruitment by blackmail.

The Soviet Union's cold war espionage program utilised every type of agent against the Western powers: highly professional "illegals", masses of part-time spies doubling as diplomatic personnel, and a seemingly endless supply of "insiders". These "insiders" included ideologically motivated agents, such as Julius and Ethel Rosenberg (though their case remains controversial), and agents whose sole motive apparently was money. A pre-eminent example of the latter is Aldrich Ames, who was paid $1.5 million to be a Soviet, and later Russian, mole in the CIA from the mid-1980s until his arrest in 1994, when he was sentenced to life in prison.

Rudolf Abel

Notorious Soviet Cold War spy [illegible]

B[illegible] Rudolf Abel [illegible]

[illegible] in 1903 [illegible] name [illegible]

[illegible] to England [illegible] later [illegible]

[illegible] In 1927 [illegible] NKVD [illegible] as an [illegible] officer for the Red [illegible] during World War II [illegible] Abel [illegible]

After World War II [illegible] the resident [illegible] the United States [illegible] which sought to [illegible] United States [illegible] trained [illegible] as well as the [illegible]

Rudolf Abel

Notorious Soviet Cold War Spy

Born as Rudolf Ivonovich Abel in Russia in 1902, although some reports indicate that he was actually born as Vilyam (Willie) Genrikhovich (August) Fisher in England, gave the name Rudolf Abel to the FBI as a way of signal to the Soviet Union that he had been captured.

Son of a metalworker, Abel moved with his family to England in 1903 and was later educated in Scotland. He spoke Russian, Yiddish, German, Polish and English (which he spoke with a Scottish accent). He served as a language instructor in the Soviet Red Army and served in Soviet Intelligence in 1930. He ultimately became language instructor for the NKVD (People's Commissariat for Internal Affairs). He served as an intelligence officer for the Red Army on the German front during World War II. He was highly decorated for battlefield services and espionage activities, including penetrating the Abwehr.

After World War II, he was selected by the KGB to serve as the resident director (or top spymaster) for Soviet espionage in the United States. He oversaw a spy network in the United States which sought to uncover United States military secrets. He was trained by the KGB in the use and repair of radio equipment, as well as the fundamentals of ciphers and codes, microdots and concealment methods. He had a background in engineering and physics as well as natural ability with photography and art.

He immigrated illegally from France to Canada in 1947 under the name Andrew Kayotis, entered the United States in 1948 under the name Emil R. Goldfus, and moved to New York City in 1949, under the code name "Mark" and used a photography studio as his headquarters. He developed a system of intelligence drops, including letterboxes and drop zones throughout New York City, oversaw the gathering of top secret intelligence information from the United Nations and U.S. military installations and managed the transfer of this information to Soviet agents or directly to Moscow. He oversaw the operations of agents Morris and Leona Cohen.

After his spy network grew too large for him to manage, Abel sought assistance from Moscow. Moscow sent agent Reino Hayhanen to serve as an intermediary, charged with collecting information from members of the spy network. He was recalled to Russia in 1955 for a six-month respite from the stressful work of overseeing the spy network in the United States.

He left the network in the hands of Hayhanen. When upon Abel's returned to the United States in 1956, the network was in shambles, due to Hayhanen's drunkenness and ineptitude. Hayhanen was recalled to Russia and fearing harsh reprimands he turned himself in to U.S authorities in France, offering to expose the entire spy network.

Exposed by Hayhanen, Abel fled New York and travelled to Florida but was immediately arrested upon his return. Charged with espionage, Abel was found guilty and sentenced to 45 years in prison. He was exchanged for U. S. U2 pilot Francis Gary Powers on February 10, 1962 on the Glieneceker Bridge, which connected East, and West Germanys. He was honoured briefly in 1965 and authored his "memoirs" in 1968, lived in relative obscurity until his death in 1971. He was honoured with a postage stamp in his likeness by the Soviet Union in 1990.

Aldrich Ames

CIA Counterintelligence Officer Convicted of Spying for Soviet Union

Aldrich Ames was born in 1941 in River Falls, Wisconsin. He was the son of Carleton Ames, a teacher at River Falls State Teachers College and grandson of Jesse Ames, the president of the school. His mother was a teacher. Carleton Ames, struggled with alcohol but introduced his son to the theatre, a passion that Aldrich would follow for years as he participated in plays throughout high school.

The Ames family moved to McLean, Virginia in 1951 when Carleton Ames took a position with the CIA where he worked for a time with James Jesus Angleton. Aldrich enrolled at George Washington University, majoring in History and took a part-time position, arranged by his father at the CIA in 1959, was believed to be one of the youngest employees ever with the agency. Eventually, he received a degree from George Washington in 1967.

He continued working with the agency and was assigned to a post in Turkey where he was sent to try to recruit new intelligence agents. Unfortunately, he was unable to recruit any new spies. He was considered aloof by those around him. This, along with his tepid performance as a case officer, caused resentment from fellow workers. He was recalled from Ankara in 1972 and assigned to a post at CIA headquarters in Langley, Virginia where he was given the task of recruiting Soviet officials. At headquarters, Ames was looked upon with disdain by his colleagues, many of whom believed that he was a product of nepotism. Despite this, he was made privy to top secret information on Soviet operatives. Still, he failed to recruit any new agents. He was assigned to the New York office

in 1980, instructed to recruit new Soviet agents from the United Nations delegation. He married his girlfriend Nancy in 1980. The couple struggled early in the marriage and Aldrich began drinking, a habit that would become problematic in the years to come.

After being passed over for a promotion (due in part to his ineptitude as a recruiter in New York), Ames applied for and was assigned to a post in Mexico City, Mexico. His wife, however, stayed behind. Met with continued lack of success as a recruiter in Mexico City, prompting him to fall further into his drinking habit. He was becoming disillusioned with certain activities by the CIA in Latin America.

He met Columbian socialite Maria del Rosario Casas, the cultural attache for the Columbian embassy in Mexico City. Her father was a former member of the Columbian Senate and she was raised in a world of privilege. She graduated Summa Cum Laude from the University of the Andes in 1974 and became a faculty member at the University shortly thereafter. She was extremely close to her mother, Cecelia Depuy de Casas, a lover of music and also a faculty member at the University. Rosario had on occasion loaned out her apartment to CIA operatives for meeting with Mexican spies. After being introduced to Ames, she was recruited by him into service with the CIA. The two were romantically involved and travelled among the more prominent circles in Mexico.

Ames was promoted in 1983, heading up the CIA Soviet counterintelligence branch, and was assigned to CIA headquarters in Langley, Virginia. In his new position, he was given access to nearly all information available on Soviet cases, including U.S. assets operating within the Soviet Union. After a period of time, he brought Rosario to the United States to live with him. She pressured him to divorce his wife Nancy and she consented, keeping most of the couples assets (the divorce was finalised in 1985). Rosario began running up huge bills, shopping and placing calls to her mother in Bogota. Ames was soon almost $60,000 in debt, but was earning only $45,000 each year. Burdened by his overwhelming debt-load, Ames began searching for means of obtaining additional money. He had once heard that a co-worker had been offered $50,000 to spy for the KGB, and he began to consider that as a possibility.

In April 1985, Ames tried to meet with Sergey Chuvakhin, a Soviet arms expert to suggest that he might be willing to spy for the Soviet Union. Instead, he decided to approach Stanislav Androsov, a Soviet agent at the Soviet embassy. Ames passed Androsov a note, offering to provide the name of three Soviets working for U.S. intelligence in exchange for $50,000. Androsov introduced him to Victor Cherkashin, the KGB counterespionage chief at the embassy. Cherkashin accepted Ames' offer and Ames was given a bag containing $50,000.

Just days after the meeting, the FBI announced the arrest of John Walker, Jr. on espionage charges. That arrest spooked Ames who feared that he could be compromised by any number of Soviet double agents. On June 13, 1985 he met with Chuvakhin and gave him the name of every double agent that he felt was in a position to expose him. He also provided a mound of CIA intelligence reports. As a result, the KGB rounded up dozens of agents, returning them to Moscow for questioning, interrogation, imprisonment and often execution.

The CIA took note that many of its double agents were disappearing and that some of their communications intelligence apparatus were no longer gathering information (including an elaborate bugging system within the tunnels running underground through Moscow). Initially, the agency believed that the activity was a result of the defection of former CIA employee Edward Lee Howard, a recent defector. Eventually they realised, however, that the information now possessed by the Soviets was outside of the scope of Howard's limited knowledge.

Although alarmed, the CIA took a cautious approach to search for a mole, still smarting from the mess stemming from James Jesus Angleton's previous mole hunt. As such, the security breach was looked upon a chance mistakes by several agents, and not the work of an internal mole.

In order to distance himself from the activities swirling around him, Ames requested a transfer to the office in Rome, Italy. While assigned there, he and his wife began spending lavishly on clothing and accessories. Ames also purchased a Jaguar.

In November 1986, the CIA assigned a 32 year employee Jeanne Vertefeuille to help isolating the source of the information flow. She and her small group of analysts focused on known traitors such as former Marine guard Clayton Lonetree, but realised that none of these people possessed the scope of knowledge apparent for the breach.

In 1987, Dan Payne, a young investigator with knowledge in accounting was assigned to her group and decided to look for a money trail to lead him to the mole. Payne began looking into the spending habits of various CIA personnel. When the Ames' moved back to the United States, they purchased an expensive house and Rosario announced to friends that she intended to add new drapes to the entire house. Knowing how expensive this would be, one of the Ames' friends, Diana Worthen, informed one of the mole hunter (Sandy Grimes), of the Ames' sudden wealth. Grimes began researching Aldrich's past dealing with the Soviets while Payne began digging through the Ames financial records and found that the couple was spending up to $30,000 each month, while Aldrich's annual salary was less than $70,000. Further investigation, however, led the CIA to believe that Rosario's family was considerably wealthy and that this was the source of the Ames' new finances.

Undeterred, Grimes continued investigating and noticed that there was a correlation between the dates of Ames meetings with Chuvakhin and his bank deposits. With this information in hand, the CIA notified the FBI, which put the Ames' under surveillance. The FBI planted bugs in Ames home, car and office. They also discovered that Ames had neglected to turn off an automated save feature in his word processor, thus leaving a trail of incriminating letters written to the Soviets. The FBI also obtained that Rosario was aware of her husband's activities and that she pressured him to continue his spying activities.

CIA officials quietly moved Ames into an area where he was not allowed to classified information. He was planning, however, to travel overseas for a conference and the FBI was worried that he might be tipped off and flee. He was summoned to work on February 21, 1994 for a routine matter but was instead intercepted and arrested by FBI agents. Rosario was simultaneously arrested at the couple's home.

Aldrich Ames offered to cooperate with the U.S. Government if they would release Rosario and not charge her with any crimes. The government, however, had enough evidence on her to prosecute so they refused the deal. Rosario was nowhere near as loving towards her husband, blaming him for deceiving and manipulating her. She was convicted and sentenced to five years in prison and was promptly deported upon her parole. She moved back to Columbia where her mother was caring for the Ames' son.

Aldrich Ames was sentenced to life in a federal prison.

James Jesus Angleton

Head of CIA Counterintelligence and Noted Mole-hunter

Born in 1916 in Boise, Idaho, James Jesus Angleton moved to Italy in 1933 when his father was transferred for business. He graduated from Yale University in 1941, entered the U.S. Army in 1943, and was placed in the Office of Strategic Services.

While working in London, was transferred into X-2, OSS' counterintelligence division. He was later transferred to Italy to head up the Italian desk of X-2. During and after the war, he cultivated friendships and contacts throughout Europe, including relationships with Kim Philby and a priest who would later become Pope Paul VI. More importantly, he became friendly with members of the Jewish underground in Europe, the forerunners of Mossad, Israel's chief intelligence service.

He joined the CIA in 1947 as one of its original officers. He also helped to establish the counterintelligence office of the CIA. He was designated to head up the Italian desk of the CIA and helped to finance the defeat of the Communist Party in the 1948 Italian general election. He was considered obsessed with the KGB and the possibility that it had infiltrated the CIA. Russian defector Anatoli Golytsin had made this claim and

Angleton followed up on it by searching for the mysterious mole from 1961 to 1974. During this time, he often dined with Kim Philby. Philby believed that Angleton was unaware that he was a Soviet spy. Angleton, however, had reported his suspicions to his superiors, years before Philby was exposed.

He enjoyed great autonomy and authority in his position, often reporting to the CIA chief at all hours. He had an enormous budget at his disposal with 300 employees working under him. He was relieved of most of his duties and power in 1974 by the new CIA chief William Colby. He was retained only as a consultant.

Colby and Angleton had had a strained relationship from the days when both worked for the OSS. Colby, in a final attempt to run Angleton out of the CIA, whispered accusations that Angleton was engaged in spying on CIA agents who were not active suspects.

After resigning from the CIA after 20 years heading up the counterespionage division, Angleton retired to a life of fly-fishing. He was awarded the CIA's highest honour, the Distinguished Intelligence Medal in 1975 and was called the "most professional counterintelligence officer" in the OSS.

Angleton died in 1987.

Josephine Baker

American-born Entertainer who Spied for France against Nazis

Born in 1906 in St. Louis, Missouri, United States, Josephine Baker became a very popular performer in musical revues on Broadway in 1924. She moved to Paris, France in 1925 to appear in the musical revue La Revue Negre. She became a citizen of France in 1937.

She was very well known for her energetic dancing and scantily clad risqué musical performances. She was one of the most well-known stars in all of Europe. She volunteered for the French Red Cross at the outbreak of the war between France and Germany in 1940. She was recruited by French Chief of Counterespionage Jacques Abtey to serve as a secret informer. After the fall of France, Baker served as a member of the French Resistance.

Relayed information to the French Resistance (as well as to British and U.S. agents) that she gleaned from conversations she overheard between German officers attending her performances. She exposed French officials working for the Germans. She also smuggled secret documents written in invisible ink on her musical sheets. She was rewarded for her actions by the French government. She was awarded the Croix de Guerre and the Medal of Resistance in 1945 and was acknowledged by U.S. General George S. Patton for her valiant efforts.

Josephine Baker died in Paris in 1975.

Lavrentiy Beria

Chief of the NKVD and Head of the Great Soviet Purge

Lavrentiy Beria was born in Merkheuli,Georgia near the Black Sea in 1899. He was drafted into the Russian Imperial Army and saw brief action during World War I before deserting in 1917 to take part in the Russian Revolution. He received an architectural degree from a technical college in Baku in 1919 but became a member of the Bolshevik Party and joined the Check, the Bolshevik Secret Police. He was sent back to his native Georgia where he spied on friends and family and anyone else who was less than supportive of the Bolshevick Revolution. As a result of his reports, hundreds of people were executed.

He quickly climbed his way up through the ranks of the Cheka, the GPU, the OGPU and later the NKVD. He ruthlesslessly blackmailed officials in order to gain political backing and promotions.

He would often set up his superiors with married women and then expose the affairs, ruining them and then taking their posts when they resigned in disgrace. He was even more ruthless with his use of violence.

He was appointed head of Soviet intelligence by V'adimir Lenin, with the backing of Josef Stalin. He was supportive in Stalin's bid for the head of the Communist Party and was rewarded by Stalin, who appointed Beria with a membership on the Central Committee of the Communist Party. Beria loyally set out to eliminate all of Stalin's potential rivals or enemies, targeted thousands of them for death. Stalin, extremely paranoid, ordered several purges of his own hitmen, including OGPU head Felix Dzerzhinsky who was killed by his successor Vyacheslav Menzhinsky, then Genrikh Yagoda and then Nicolai

Yezhov. Stalin feared that each bloodthirsty liquidator that he empowered was more powerful than him. Beria was yet another of these murderers and in one of his first actions upon ascending to the head of the NKVD, Lavrenti ordered the execution of five officials high in command in the Ukraine.

He gave the order for the assassination of Leon Trotsky, an exile in Mexico in 1940.

He was named Deputy Prime Minister in February 1941, in charge of Russian security after the invasion by the Germans. He used this opportunity to murder as many old Bolsheviks as he could, thus eliminating as many of Stalin's old political rivals. He began a horrific purge, going so far as to order the mass execution of more than 10,000 political prisoners he had sent to detention camps.

He was named a member of the State Defense Committee and Marshall of the Soviet Union in 1945. He was made a full member of the Soviet Politburo in 1946. He was eventually put in charge of Atomic bomb development.

He was viewed by many as a distasteful monster, believed to be a sexual predator, accused of raping and sodomising young girls and threatening their families to keep them quiet. He gave the NKVD a makeover, renaming it the MVD. In addition to massive internal investigations and purges, Beria oversaw the implementation of a worldwide espionage system, aimed at gathering intelligence from the west.

As had happened with his predecessors, Beria fell out of favour with Stalin due to Stalin's continued paranoia. Stalin, feeling Beria possessed too much power, feared that his top policeman would attempt to overthrow him. Believing that Beria had set in motion a plot to assassinate him, Stalin ordered him arrestes. Stalin died soon thereafter (some believe Stalin suffered a stroke while speaking alone with Beria).

Beria allegedly began making his move for control. He pushed a political ally into the position of Soviet premier and himself assumes the position of Vice Chairman of the Council of Ministers and then eased political sanctions throughout the Soviet union, setting himself up as a more liberal leader. In June 1953, however, Beria, who had made many enemies, was labelled a traitor and by the orders of Khruschev he was convicted by the Soviet Supreme Court and executed by a firing squad on December 23, 1953 at the Lubianka Prison.

George Blake

British Spy who Worked as a Double Agent for Soviet Union

Born George Behar in 1922 in Rotterdam, Holland, the son of wealthy parents who provided him with a private school education, his father died in 1936. George Blake was sent to an exclusive school at his father's earlier behest, when he died in 1936. He was cared for by his aunt and lived with her family (her husband and son). He learnt English at his new school.

George's cousin Henri Curiel, Jr. eventually founded the Communist Party in Egypt and helped influence George's movement towards communism. George returned to Rotterdam in 1938 attending high school until Nazi occupation of the Netherlands. He sent much of his family fleeing to England. George, who was half-Jewish, fought the occupation as part of the Dutch underground movement. After being captured, he escaped from an internment camp in which he was placed. A harbinger of things to come, Blake fled to England, by way of France and Spain.

He joined the British Royal Navy under the name George Blake, entering the Special Operations Executive unit where he served as an interpreter and translated German documents. Following the war, enrolled in Cambridge University, where he studied Russian.

After finishing college, Blake joined the British Foreign Office and was assigned to the British Embassy in South Korea. He was captured by Communist troops when the Korean War broke out and was interned for three years and subjected to frequent brainwashing sessions. He escaped the internment camp but was quickly recaptured. He was about to be executed as a spy when he shouted aloud in Russian that he was not a spy. One of the guards understood Russian and had a discussion with him about Communism. He was returned to the camp and released soon after.

Upon his release, he was transferred to MI6 in order to work as a secret agent. Despite a standing rule that only citizens of British parentage were eligible for acceptance into MI6, Rotterdam born Blake was accepted anyway.

After being exposed in 1961 by a Polish defector, Blake was arrested by SIS agents. After thorough questioning, Blake provided a full confession and was subsequently charged with violating the Official Secrets Act. British agents were horrified to discover that Blake was one of the most damaging spies in Britain's history and he was quickly convicted and sentenced to 42 years in Wormwood Scrubs Prison.

Escaped from Wormwood in 1966, breaking out of his cell window and then climbing a makeshift ladder supplied by a former prison colleague, Sean Bourke, who then drove Blake to safety. Making his way through East Germany, he eventually reached Moscow where he met his fellow spies Gordon Lonsdale, Kim Philby and Donald MacLean.

Anthony Blunt

Noted British Art Historian who Acted as a Soviet Recruiter

Born in Bournemouth, England in 1907, Anthony Blunt was the son of an English clergyman.

He moved to Paris with his family in 1911 but returned to England where he graduated from Cambridge University in 1932. He became a Fellow at Trinity College and recruited numerous students into his espionage activities, including Kim Philby, David MacLean and Guy Burgess, with whom Blunt was sexually involved (Blunt, Philby, MacLean and Burgess were four members of the Cambridge Five, England's most notorious spy ring).

He served in the British Army during World War II, and was stationed in France. He again came to France after the

Nazi occupation of France and worked as a counterintelligence officer under MI5 and from 1940 to 1945, conveyed documents and top secret information to Soviet handlers. He left MI5 at the end of the war and began developing his career in the area of art history. He became one of the foremost authorities in the field, receiving numerous awards and titles, most notably a Fellow of the British Academy, a professor of Art History at the University of London and was knighted by Queen Elizabeth in 1956.

It is believed by many that he tipped off Kim Philby about the impending arrest of Donald MacLean which lead MacLean and Burgess to flee to the Soviet Union. He was accused of being a spy for the Soviet Union in 1964 by Arthur Martin. Evidence was supplied by an American, Michael Whitney, who claimed that Blunt had recruited him as a KGB agent in the 1930's. He admitted to being the "Fourth Man", but bargained for his freedom by promising to reveal all of his activities and knowledge about espionage activities by the Soviet Union. British officials decided to keep his involvement quiet in order to prevent a scandal regarding a knight of Britain.

He was publicly exposed after the British press investigated his possible involvement in espionage. After the book "The Climate of Treason" by Andrew Boyle was published, British Prime Minister Margaret Thatcher was questioned as to the identity of the "Fourth Man". Thatcher identified Blunt by name, during a session of Parliament. He was stripped of his knighthood, titles and prestigious positions. He lived out the rest of his life quietly in disgrace and died in 1983.

John Cairncross

British Intelligence Officer who Passed Secrets to Soviet Union

Born in 1913 in Scotland, John Cairncross was highly educated, attending Glasgow University and obtaining degrees in French and German at the Sorbonne in France before entering Cambridge University on scholarship to study modern languages.

He was introduced to Anthony Blunt and Guy Burgess and soon became a Communist working with the Cambridge Spy Ring. Monitored by Soviet agent Samuel Cahan, he received a short course in espionage tactics before taking the Home Office and Foreign Office exams, receiving the highest scores on both.

He was assigned to the Foreign Office in 1936 where he worked briefly with Donald Maclean. He served briefly as the personal secretary to Lord Maurice Hankey who oversaw Intelligence services in Britain then moved on to the Bletchley Code and Cipher School. In the course of his job, he passed intercepted messages and other classified information to his Soviet handler. He often delivered cases full of intercepted German messages in the back seat of his car which he drove to the Soviet embassy.

During World War II, he worked for MI6 in its London headquarters, and smuggled plans for postwar Yugoslavia to the Soviets. After World War II, he continued to pass information to Soviet agents, including Kim Philby, Donald Maclean and Guy Burgess.

In 1951, sensitive documents in Cairncross' handwriting were found in Burgess apartment after Burgess and Maclean fled to Russia. He was thus fired from his position in the British Treasury department, although he denied being a spy. He turned to scholarly activities and humanitarian efforts for the United Nations.

In 1964, Sir Anthony Blunt confessed to being a Soviet spy and in return for leniency identified Cairncross as another Soviet agent. When confronted with the evidence, Cairncross admitted to his espionage, explaining that he had not spied for several years, saying that he spied only during World War II, when Russia was a British ally.

Soviet defectors later disputed Cairncross statements about his limited involvement in espionage. They claimed that he had turned over countless reams of information.

Fearful of negative publicity and scandal, the British government hushed up his activities, declining to prosecute him for espionage or to expose him to the public. Cairncross, in fact, remained for a time in his job as with the United Nations Food and Agricultural Organisation.

Cairncross was exposed in 1981 by Prime Minister Margaret Thatcher. He continued his life in exile until 1995 when he moved to Britain and married American opera singer Gayle Brinkerhoff. Later that year, he died after suffering a stroke.

Whittaker Chambers

American-born Soviet Spy who Exposed Alger Hiss as a Spy

Whittaker Chamber was born in 1901 in Philadelphia, Pennsylvania. He was the son of a journalist.

He attended Columbia University, beginning in 1920 but was expelled in 1922 for writing a play that was deemed "blasphemous" by the University. He joined the American Communist Party in 1925 and became a writer for its main publication *the Daily Worker*. He married Esther Shemitz, herself a Communist, in 1931. His wife got him involved with the Communist underground movement seeking to overthrow the United States government. Chambers moved to Baltimore in 1934, using the name George Crosleyas, he delivered stolen classified documents to a Russian agent, Colonel Boris Bykov.

After becoming disillusioned with Communism and the party, Chambers left the ACP. In 1939 after watching the signing of the non-aggression agreement between the Soviet Union and Germany, Chambers decided to approach U.S. officials and tell them what he knew about Soviet espionage efforts within the U.S. Having found employment with Time magazine, he turned to another journalist named Isaac Dan Levine who introduced him to the Assistant Secretary of State Adolf Berle whose position involved national security. Chambers confessed his actions to Berle and told him of other Soviet controlled agents working within the U.S. government and government installations. Chambers exposed mathematician Franklin Reno an employee at the Aberdeen Proving Grounds (home to bomb and explosives research), as well as Colonel Bykov.

He also cast light on Alger Hiss, former State Department official and former Director General of the United Nations. Chambers claimed that Hiss was a Communist and had served as a high level spy within the State Department for years. The allegations about Hiss were relayed to the highest level of government, the Oval Office of the White House, where President Franklin Roosevelt was purported to have laughed at the allegation as preposterous. The matter was dropped and Chambers returned to Time magazine where he was promoted to the position of Senior Editor in 1948.

On August 3, 1948, Chambers was called before the House Un-American Activities Committee and reiterated his allegations. He again focused on Alger Hiss. Hiss offered to appear before the committee to deny the charges and was called in on August 5, 1948.

Hiss stated that what Chambers was saying was absolutely untrue and challenged Chambers' veracity. Furthermore, Hiss stated that he had never been a Communist and had never even met Chambers. The committee recalled Chambers and told him of Hiss' rebuke. Chambers began revealing specific details about Hiss and his family. His information about the family's personal information was so detailed and so specific, it became apparent that it could only have been obtained through personal knowledge. When Hiss was recalled, he confirmed much of what Chambers had stated about the Hiss family and then acknowledged that he may have known Chambers before, but under his assumed name of George Crosley, when his appearance was different. Chambers later appeared on the Meet the Press television show and reiterated his belief that Hiss was indeed a Communist spy. Hiss sued him for slander.

The Committee turned up more evidence that seemed to support Chambers' allegations and Chambers provided more information to support his claims. Chambers produced film of photographs of classified documents from the State Department that he claimed had been retyped by Hiss' wife. Furthermore, Chambers directed authorities to his farm property where he had hidden more undeveloped film in a hollowed-out pumpkin. Hiss was subsequently indicted for perjury for claiming not to have known Chambers after July 1935. The trial began on May 31, 1949 and the prosecution entered into evidence the Hiss' typewriter that seemed to match directly with the type in the retyped documents. After the trial resulted in a hung jury, Hiss was retried in November 1949 and was convicted in January 1950 and sentenced to five years in prison. (Hiss was never charged with espionage.) For the rest of his life, Hiss attempted to overturn his conviction but met with little success.

Chambers faded away from the public eye and died in July 1961. In 1984, President Ronald Reagan awarded Chambers the Medal of Freedom, the highest civilian honour in the United States.

Morris Childs

An American-born Soviet Spy who Later Became a Double Agent Working for the United States

Morris Childs was born as Moishe Chilovsky in Kiev in 1902. He grew up in Chicago, changed his name to Morris Childs and took part in a growing left wing movement within the city. He became one of the charter members of the American Communist Party in 1919.

In 1929, he was selected by the Soviet Communist Party to attend the prestigious Lenin School in Moscow where he learned about the concepts of developing revolution and the fundamental principles of Communism. Among his schoolmates were future Soviet premiers Nikita Khrushchev and Leonid Brezhnev and Morris Ponomarov who would go on to serve as a member of the politburo and as the international head of the Communist Party.

Childs headed the Illinois district of the American Communist Party, a key position and ran for the United States Senate seat under the political wing of the Communist Party. He gathered only 1,000 votes. He served as the editor of the Daily Worker, the leading communist publication in the United States. He was considered to be one of the leading figures in the Communist movements in the United States. He was replaced as editor of the Daily Worker due to political machinations between rival components of the American Communist Party. He was weakened by the movement and crumbled under the stress and strain, suffering a debilitating heart attack in 1947. He felt abandoned when no one from the Communist Party offered aid or comfort. A deep resentment over his ouster from his prominent position within the American Communist Party combined with his feelings of abandonment during his medical crisis caused an overwhelming sense of betrayal to brew within him.

After numerous raids on American Communist Party leaders in the United States by the FBI, the Justice Department sought to destroy the party from within by seeking disillusioned members of the group. Because of his ill health and his loss of position, the FBI targeted Morris and his brother Jack as ideal candidates to work as informants. Morris was approached by FBI agent Carl Freyman who found that Morris was not only angry over his betrayal by the American Communist Party, but has also become disillusioned with the Communist mantra, especially in light of the egregious actions of Soviet dictator Stalin. Morris agreed to work with the FBI to gather information about the Communist Party. The U.S. Government provided medical treatment for Morris and he soon regained his health. He was assigned the title Agent CG5824S but was referred to internally as "58". Because the hope was that Morris would travel alone into the Soviet Union in a quest for information, the involvement was deemed "Operation Solo".

After two years of working his way back into the American Communist fold, Morris was summoned to a meeting where he was instructed to travel to Russia to arrange for financing of the American Communist Party by the Soviets. Travelled to the Soviet Union in April 1958 and met with his old friend Morris Ponomarov who deemed Childs the real United States ambassador. The two devised a plan by which to smuggle Soviet funds into the United States, using Morris' brother Jack as a courier. Over 30 years, the Childs brothers would facilitate the transfer of more than $30 million, which was then disbursed by Morris throughout the United States to different American communist causes (with the FBI, of course, monitoring the activity. The FBI took an inventory of the money and traced its origins, determining that a significant amount of it flowed in from Cuba).

In 1959, Childs travelled back in to the Soviet Union to attend a meeting of all heads of state of communist nations. Serving as the U.S. delegate, he was elected recording secretary and thereby obtained privy to top secret documents. One night while filing away some of these documents in his safe, he slammed the door on his little finger, cutting the tip of it off. Fearful that under sedation he might reveal that he was working on behalf of the FBI, he refused an anaesthetic and had the doctors stitch him up. The next day, Premier Khrushchev acknowledged the incident, boasting that Morris was so committed that he refused the anaesthetic because he was so protective of the Soviet documents that he would endure the great pain rather than possibly betray the state secrets. Khrushchev called Childs to the podium before a crowded assembly and affectionately announced him to the "the last of the true Bolsheviks". This solidified his role as a highly trusted member of Khrushchev's inner circle and legitimised his position within the Kremlin. Because of the heights within which Childs had ascended within the Soviet power-base, Operation Solo was one of the most protected secrets within the Department of Justice. Only 12 people knew of Childs role and of the operation. In fact, not a single President of the United States knew about it until Gerald Ford was in office.

He married Eva Lieb in 1962 and revealed his role as an agent of the FBI. Eva participated in the clandestine activities as well as providing moral support to Morris who often found himself under overwhelming stress. Morris travelled back to Moscow in November 1963 and was visiting with Ponomarov when news arrived of the assassination of President John Kennedy. Childs, who understood Russian fluently (a fact that he kept from the Soviets) listened in to a conversation between Ponomarov and a KGB official. From this Childs learned that the Soviet Union had nothing to do with the assassination. While in Moscow, Childs would bring home sensitive files which he and Eva would copy in the dark of night. Eva then smuggled these copies inside her blouse back to the United States.

Informed the FBI that Stanley Levison had been a financial advisor for the Communist Party of the United States in 1954. Although Levison dropped out of the party a few years later, FBI Director J. Edgar Hoover became alarmed because Levison had become an advisor of civil rights leader Martin Luther King, Jr. in the 1960's. Hoover, infatuated with King, sought to paint King as a communist working under the guidance of Levison. When the FBI informed King of Levison's past, King refused to disassociate himself from his advisor. This resulted in Hoover bugging King's home and hotel rooms. Hoover attempted to blackmail King with evidence of alleged adulterous affairs, an activity which caused horrific negative fallout upon the Bureau.

In January 1967, Childs made his 22nd trip to the Soviet Union on behalf of the FBI, he was confronted by Ponomarov with information obtained by a Soviet spy who had come across an FBI file which documented some of the information from Operation Solo, information that only Childs should have been privy to. Childs, in grave danger, bluffed his way out claiming that there must have been a leak in the Communist Party USA.

Childs, because of his position in the Communist Party also met with communist dignitaries around the world, including Chairman Mao Tse-tung of China. He learned that the Soviet Union and China were not friendly allies, despite their communist beliefs. He reported this divide, allowing the United States to develop a relationship with China during the Richard Nixon presidency.

In 1977, returning from his 57th trip to Moscow as an FBI informant, Morris and Eva were stunned when the plane they were on was ordered back to Moscow immediately. Sensing the worst, the couple prepared for the most dire consequences. Fortunately, the plane was called back only because Communist Party USA head Gus Hall had arrived in Moscow and wanted to meet with Childs. After their meeting, Childs and Eva safely returned to the United States. In 1980, fearful that the Church Commission's investigation had put the Childs' at too much risk, Morris and Eva were given new identities and Operation Solo was shut down. In 1988, Morris was quietly awarded the National Security Medal by FBI Director William Sessions.

Morris Childs died in 1991 and his wife Eva died four years later. He is only now being recognised officially for his contributions as perhaps the most important spy in the history of the United States as he served as the FBI's eyes and ears in the Kremlin for almost forty years.

Morris "Two-Gun" Cohen

London-born Adventurer who Arranged Counterintelligence for China

Born in London in 1889. Morris Cohen spent much of his early life which involved brushes with the law. He was sent to reform school and was sent to live with relatives in Canada after his release.

He took in various jobs but exhibited an immense talent as a gambler. After accumulating vast earnings from his talents, he was able to get associated with members of high society. One such affair was his introduction to Chinese revolutionary Sun Yet-sen. Yet-sen was leading a revolt against the Manchu dynasty, trying to supplant it with a unified China, complete with western-based democracy. Yet-sen had brokered deals which provided him with sufficient funds to lead the revolution but was having trouble securing arms for fighting.

Cohen suggested that he could fully arm the revolutionaries and was engaged to do so. His success in doing so prompted Yet-sen to bring Cohen in as a trusted advisor after the revolution's success in 1912. Cohen accepted the invitation and after the end of

World War I, travelled to China and was named the Head of Intelligence for Yet-sen in 1922.

Established an elaborate counter-espionage system, reporting to Yet-sen events and activities within China as well as Japan. Employed two spies, Isaac Lincoln and Lionel Philip Kenneth Crabb, both of whom were known for the adventurous exploits.

Often engaged in hand to hand combat in beating down insurrection movements against Yet-sen. At all times, he wore a gun in his shoulder holster and one in a hip holster (thus earning the nickname "Two-Gun") and often led the charge into enemy lines. He devised methods of intelligence gathering, establishing sophisticated networks involving common farmers in various provinces of China as well as foreign diplomats and businessmen. He employed various levels of interrogation to extract information from captured enemies, including torture and execution.

After Yet-sun's death in 1925, Cohen assumed the same role with Chiang Kai-shek, Yet-sen's successor. He worked vigorously to gather information about the Chinese Communist Party which was gaining a foothold in China. Likewise, obtained information from people close to Japanese military intelligence. He learnt that Japanese military intelligence officer Major Ryukichi Tanaka and his mistress Eastern Jewel planned to create a violent disturbance in Shanghai in order to provide

Japan with an excuse to attack and invade the city. He warned Kai-shek, but was taken prisoner by the Japanese in Hong Kong.

He was released by the Japanese after the end of World War II. Upon his return, found that he had been replaced. He had lost his position and left China. He eventually returned to Canada where he died in 1970.

Judith Coplon

American-born Soviet Agent who Passed Information about American Counterintelligence

Born in Brooklyn, New York in 1922. Judith Coplon was the daughter of a prominent manufacturer.

She graduated Cum Laude from Barnhard College in 1943, having focused on Russian History and Culture and was employed by the United States Department of Justice, first in New York and later in Washington D.C. after being promoted to the foreign agents registration division. She had access to FBI documents with lists of foreign diplomats and suspected foreign spies. She was highly praised for her analysis on Soviet political and cultural issues. She got promotions at regular intervals.

She started supplying information to the Soviets sometime between 1945 and 1947 and was assigned a special Soviet contact, an Intelligence Officer named Valentin Gubitchev. Gubitchev was a former member of the Soviet delegation to the United Nations. At the time he started meeting Coplon, he was an employee for the United Nations.

In 1948, an unidentified informant passed information along to the Director of the Federal Bureau of Investigation J. Edgar Hoover, reporting that a woman, formerly employed in the New York branch but then working at the Washington offices of the Department of Justices was passing secrets that were making their way to the Russian Embassy in New York.

She often travelled to New York City on the weekends, often asked to leave from work early on Fridays. She took classified documents home with her and retyped them and gave the retyped documents to Gubitchev when she visited him in New York.

She requested a special document containing a list of suspected Soviet spies. Director Hoover personally delivered a fake version of the document to Coplon's supervisor, who immediately provided it to her. Coplon, upon receiving the document requested the rest of the day off and then travelled to New York for the weekend (followed by FBI agents – January 14, 1949).

She was trailed by FBI agents around Manhattan until she finally met with Gubitchen in a restaurant. After exchanging documents, the couple left and boarded a subway train. As the doors to the train were closing, Gubitchev bolted from the train and evaded the trailing FBI agents.

Having been observed passing documents, Coplon was transferred to another division of the Department of Justice, in order to keep her away from sensitive documents. Coplon continued to seek access to such documents, volunteering to aid her replacement in getting up to speed.

She requested additional classified information that her supervisor had recently obtained (fake information received from Hoover). Her supervisor left the information in Coplon's view and left the room. Coplon left the room and caught a train to New York (March 6, 1949).

After meeting Gubitchev, Coplon and her Soviet handler were confronted by FBI agents. After trying to flee, both were apprehended and arrested. Coplon had numerous top-secret documents on her person, including the one provided by Hoover. Coplon was charged with treason and espionage and Gubitchev was charged with espionage.

Coplon faced two trials, one in Washington and one in New York. She was convicted in both. Gubitchev was convicted and deported. Coplon convictions were overturned, as an Appeals Court ruled that the FBI had illegally recorded conversations between Coplon and her attorney and further that the FBI had arrested her without an arrest warrant.

She married one of her attorneys and moved to New York where she settled down as a housewife.

Lionel Crabb

British Royal Navy Diver Assigned to Missions against the Soviet Union

Lionel Crabb was born January 28, 1909 in Streatham, London.

Crabb and his mother Beatrice and father Hugh lived in poverty. Nicknamed "Buster", Crabb served as a merchant seaman as World War II began and was commissioned into the Royal Navy Patrol Service in 1941 after first serving as an army gunner. Because of an eye injury he was unable to travel to sea and volunteered for the dangerous task of mine and bomb disposal. He was assigned to Gibraltar in 1942 and aided other Navy divers in protecting British ships against Italian saboteurs. Italian frogmen ambitiously sought to install limpet mines to the hulls of British ships.

Initially, Crabb was assigned to disarm bomb removed from ships, but he eventually asked to be trained as a diver. He was a quick learner and received numerous commendations, including a George Medal. He was eventually promoted to the rank of Lieutenant Commander. He became the Principal Diving Officer for Northern Italy in 1943. A few years later, he was stationed to Palestine and in 1948 he left the Royal Navy.

For a few years Crabb was in the private sector working for the Atomic Weapons Research Establishment at Aldermaston. He also worked with searching through sunken Spanish galleons.

In 1952, Crabb returned to active duty and was assigned to frogman duties in various ports. He searched and investigated sunken Royal Navy submarines. He married Margaret Player and continued on as a frogman, and in 1955 worked with another frogman, Sydney Knowles, investigated the hull of a Soviet ship, the Sverdlov.

Crabb was recruited by MI6 and on April 19, 1956, he was assigned to perform surveillance on a Soviet cruiser. The cruiser, the Ordzhonikidze, had carried Soviet premier Nikolai Bulganin and future premier Nikita Khrushchev into Portsmouth Harbour in England on a diplomatic mission. Crabb was inspecting the hull of the ship but did not check in with his MI6 contact. He was never seen again.

On June 9, 1957, a body was found in a frogman outfit off the coast of Pilsey Island. The body was missing its head and both hands and thus made identification impossible. Neither Margaret Player (the two has divorced years earlier) nor his girlfriend, Pat Rose, could identify him. A subsequent examination by a coroner announced that it was most likely Crabb's.

Speculation swirled around Crabb's disappearance. Rumours abounded that he was captured by the Soviets, that he was a double agent and defected to the Soviet union and even that he was shot by the British services. However, in 1990, Joseph Zwerkin, a former Soviet Intelligence agent explained that Soviet security saw Crabb as he was inspecting the Ordzhonikidze and a sniper shot him in the water. The fallout from the disappearance was immense. Crabb was operating under the guidance of MI6 which is governed to operate outside of Britain while MI5 operates within the country. Although MI6 attempted to cover-up the operation, British Prime Minister Anthony Eden forced the resignation of John Alexander Sinclair, the Director-General of MI6.

British government documents related to the Crabb case will not be released until 2057.

Velvalee Dickinson

American Businesswoman who Passed U.S. Naval Secrets to the Japanese

Born in 1893 in Sacramento, California, Velvalee Dickinson was the daughter of wealthy southern parents. She attended high school in Sacramento and then attended Stanford University, graduating in 1917.

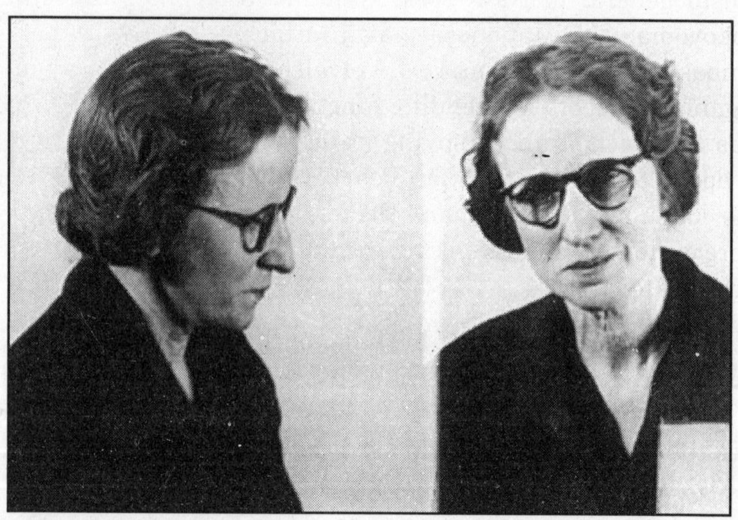

She worked as an accountant for a brokerage house run by Lee Dickinson. Velvalee married Lee and both worked servicing Japanese-American truck drivers and farmers. Because of a significant growth in the produce business in the area, Lee Dickinson opened a branch office of his company in 1932. The Dickinsons became acquainted with numerous Japanese diplomatic and military officials and became active in a number of Japanese-American organisations.

The brokerage house failed due to the economic climate of the great depression and the couple was forced to move to New York in 1935. Velvalee took a job selling dolls in Bloomingdale, dolls having been a hobby of hers as a child. In 1938, she opened her own doll shop on Madison Avenue and met with enormous success. Her clientele included famous socialites and movies stars and Velvalee became known as an expert on dolls and their clothing and accessories. In addition to her doll shop, she established a large mail-order business as well.

She re-established ties with the Japanese-American community. She was particularly friendly with the Japanese consul general in New York, Kaname Wakasugi, and Tchira Yokoyoma, the Japanese naval attache for the Japanese Embassy in Washington, D.C. Velvalee joined several Japanese organisations, often attending functions in Japanese attire. She was approached about spying on behalf of Japan and agreed to do so. After the attack on Pearl Harbour in December 1941, she lost contact with many of her Japanese associates, who were either under surveillance by the U.S. Government or were expelled to Japan.

She travelled with her husband back and forth between the east and west coast of the United States, assessing the strength of various naval stations and vessels within. They were funded by Japanese intelligence and used the cover of looking browsing the west coast for dolls and other antiques to sell.

Used a delivery system for passing coded messages. These letters were sent to Senora Inez Lopez deMalinali, in Buenos Aires, Argentina and were sent, obstensively from various women in the New York area. Each letter contained fairly innocuous information, often mentioning dolls. The dolls were a code name for a specific warship and the attire or accessories were used to indicate its origin (for instance, a doll in a hula skirt would refer to a warship from Hawaii had arrived in California).

The contact in Buenos Aires had her cover blown and fled but Japanese intelligence failed to inform Dickinson of this. When the letters were returned to the United States as undeliverable, several of the women who allegedly sent them contacted postal authorities. The FBI became involved and determined that the alleged "senders" were all clients of Dickinson's doll shop. The FBI allowed her to continue on, hoping to use her to track others in the spy chain.

Lee Dickinson died of a heart attack in March 1943. Authorities finally descended upon her in January 1944 and arrested her at her doll shop, finding a large amount of money in her safety deposit box that could be traced to a Japanese bank in New York. She was indicted on espionage charges and for violating censorship laws. She was convicted for censorship violations and sentenced to 10 years in prison and a $10,000 fine and sent to a correctional facility in Alderson, West Virginia. She was paroled in 1951 and disappeared in February 1954.

Nelson Drummond

U.S. Naval Clerk Coerced into Turning over Secret Documents to the Soviets

Nelson Drummond served as a yeoman first class at the U.S. Naval Headquarters in London, England in the mid-1950's. He worked as a clerk and had access to top secret documents and received NATO and "Cosmic" clearance.

He was a heavy drinker and often found himself in financial difficulties due to heavy gambling debts. He was approached one evening in a tavern by a KGB agent who offered to buy him a drink. Drummond accepted and the agent continued buying drinks all night. The agent later asked the drunken Drummond if he would obtain a Naval identification card for the agent, for use at the Naval Exchange store. Drummond agreed and accepted $250 for his efforts, signing a receipt slip for having received the cash.

He was immediately blackmailed, with the KGB threatening to show the receipt to Naval authorities if he refused to cooperate in turning over documents to them. Drummond did as they demanded, supplying the Russians with sensitive documents in return for payments of cash.

He was transferred to the United States in 1958, but continued supplying to the Soviets from his numerous ports of travel (at various times he was stationed in Norfolk , Virginia, Boston, Massachusetts and Newport, Rhode Island). Many of these documents included training and operating manuals, a large number of which he stole from the Newport Naval Base (the information he passed concerned naval weapons systems and antisubmarine electronics, he turned these documents over to Russian diplomats working out of the United Nations.

He continued his espionage activities until 1964, when the FBI was alerted to his actions. Drummond made a full confession, estimating that he had received upwards of $20,000 over the period of time. His activities cost the United States more than $200 million, the cost of replacing and revising the documents, manuals and plans he had turned over to the KGB,

He was convicted and sentenced to life in prison, the first Black American ever convicted of espionage.

Paul Dukes

M16 Officer Assigned to Spy on Russia Utilising Assorted Disguises

Born in London, England in 1889, the son of a clergyman, Paul Dukes was educated in Surrey and graduated from Charterhouse in 1909. He continued his education at St. Petersburg, Russia, where he studied music at the prestigious observatory and later worked as the assistant to the conductor of the Imperial Marinsky Opera. He took a job in 1916 with the Anglo-Russian Commission, reporting on the Russian press. The Anglo-Russian Commission coordinated the war efforts of the two countries during World War I.

He began working for the British government as a spy in 1918 and met with MI6 head Mansfield Cummings. He was given a brief training in espionage but was hurriedly sent to Russia where he monitored the turbulent activities surrounding the Russian Revolution and the rise of the Bolshevik party. He employed a number of disguises and covers as he worked from deep within, assessing the strength of the fragile, new Bolshevik government. He recommended the British government support the White Russians, a group opposing the Bolshevik regimes and working towards its overthrow. Dukes went so far as to row in a small boat into the Baltic Sea where he met with British patrol ships.

He was made a spymaster within Russia, working with the National Center, an organisation representing the White Russians. Dukes helped to finance this group and its soldiers with money received from Britain (although much of the money he received from England was counterfeit).

Feliks Dzerzhinsky

Head of the Bolshevik Secret Police, the CHEKA

Born in Vilna, Lithuania in 1877, Feliks Dzerzhinsky wanted to become a priest at an early age, but became involved in politics as a teenager and helped to lead protests against the czarist regime in Russia at the time. He was arrested several times from 1897 to 1900 and twice escape from the Siberian prison to which he was confined.

He continued to work as a political agitator in Berlin, Germany and in Poland. He was again arrested and imprisoned. Twice more he was imprisoned for the same charge and in 1917 was released from prison by the Bolsheviks during the Russian Revolution.

He was a trusted ally of Vladimir Lenin and was placed in charge of security for senior party members. He was later appointed by Lenin to serve as the head of Cheka, the Russian Secret Police (and precursor to the KGB). Cheka consisted of less than 25 employees when it was established but boasted more than 37,000 just two years later.

Cheka was designed as three divisions. The First Directorate was concerned with detecting and putting down subversive activities within the Soviet Union, the Second Directorate with subversive was active outside the Soviet borders and the Third Directorate looking for the same within the Soviet military system.

Designed and developed a ruthless, merciless, brutal system of eliminating political dissidents. Employed imprisonment, torture and murder without hesitation, both to set an example and as a precautionary measure. Sanctioned assassinations abroad as well as planted the seeds of intelligence networks throughout Europe and within the United States.

He setup the first Soviet concentration camps in Solovetsky Island in 1922 and also served as the first Director of Transportation for the Soviet Union, overseeing the reorganisation of the Russian Railway system.

In 1924, he was named Director of the Soviet Economics Council. He died on July 20, 1926, reportedly by natural causes, although speculation exists that he suffered a fatal stroke while engaged in an argument with Josef Stalin.

Klaus Fuchs

German-born British Theoretical Physicist and Atomic Spy

The son of Lutheran pastor, Klaus Fuchs was born in 1911 in Russelheim, Germany. He rose to power very fast and stayed at the peak for a long time.

Fuchs was raised in a very religiously strict home, with fervent anti-Nazi overtones. He got his education at the University of Leipzig. He was an organiser of the German Socialist Party. He joined the Communist Party as a student at the University of Kiel but fled to England when Adolph Hitler attained power in September 1933. He obtained a Ph.D. from the University of Bristol in 1936 and followed that up with a Sc.D. from the University of Edinburgh.

He attempted to become a British citizen in 1939, but England entered World War II against Germany and Fuchs was arrested as a suspected German agent (which he was not). He was sent to an internment camp in Canada. He became extremely angry and resentful of his treatment by the British and was likely contacted by Soviet agents during this time. He was released from the internment camp based in part on his noted anti-Nazi statements. Based on his background and capabilities in physics, was recruited back to England to work on the joint effort between England and the United States to create the atomic bomb. After obtaining security clearance, worked with Professor Rudolf Peierlson an endeavour called the Tube Alloys Project. While working on this atomic research, he also became a British citizen.

Although working on the atomic bomb research project for Britain, developed a moral dilemma in that he felt the Soviet Union should have access to the same research, being an ally with Britain and the United States. He developed a contact with the Soviet Embassy in London and agreed to pass on information. He started his mission by delivering copies of monthly reports to his contact, Semion Kremer.

He was sent by Britain to the United States to work further on the atomic research project in late 1943 at Columbia University. He met a new Soviet contact in the United States named Harry Gold (known to Fuchs as Raymond). He delivered research notes to Gold each month, while in New York and later after being transferred to the Los Alamos laboratories in New Mexico where actual development of the bomb took place. Stepped up the meetings with Gold, delivering information each week to him.

He delivered technical schematics of the atomic bomb as well as reports on test blasts. He delivered information about an experimental plutonium bomb. He ended his meetings with Gold after the United States dropped atomic bombs on Hiroshima and Nagasaki.

After returning to England in 1946, Fuchs served as the head of the theoretical physics division of the Atomic Energy Establishment in Harwell. England was in the process of developing its own atomic weapon and wanted Fuchs contributing to the effort. He continued to supply the Soviet embassy with documents and information, keeping them abreast of British innovations, despite the fact that World War II had ended.

He was assigned a new contact in Britain, code-named "Sonia". Sonia was in fact Ruth Kuczynski, a very successful Soviet spy throughout Europe. Sonia proved to be a difficult taskmaster, more and more demanding of Fuchs for information.

Fuchs became disenchanted with Soviet requests, believing that their use of the information was nowhere near as noble as he had envisioned. Eventually, severed contact with Sonia any Soviet agents.

In 1949, the FBI uncovered information detailing the actions of a scientist working on the Los Alamos project, active in disseminating classified information to foreign agents. The scientist, code-named "CHARL'Z" was determined to be Fuchs, the FBI informed British Intelligence liaison Kim Philby (himself a member of the notorious Cambridge spy ring). Philby, afraid of exposing his own espionage activities, passed the information along to British authorities, but lacking hard evidence, Britain was unable to arrest Fuchs.

Ignorant of the investigation centered on him, Fuchs approached a Harwell security officer to inquire as to concerns regarding his father's recent appointment at the University of Leipzig in Soviet-controlled East Germany. MI5 sent William Skardon, one of their top interrogators to interview him. Under friendly questioning, Fuchs broke down and confessed on January 27, 1950. In his confession, Fuchs implicated several spies, including Harry Gold. Exposing Gold in turn exposed David Greenglass, which in turn, exposed Julius Rosenberg and his wife Ethel.

Later on Fuchs was tried for violating the Official Secrets Act. He explained his actions by claiming a "controlled schizophrenia" which allowed him to value the Marxist philosophy and passing secrets to the Soviets while at the same time holding a loyalty to England. The court was unimpressed and sentenced Fuchs to 14 years in prison.

He was sent to the Wormwood Scrubs prison where he served as the prison librarianm, but was released in 1959 after serving as a model prisoner. Moved to East Germany and headed the Central Institute for Nuclear Physics in Dresden.

Fuchs married Greta Keilson and lived in relative anonymity until his death, by natural causes, in 1988.

❖❖❖

Igor Gouzenko

Soviet Cipher Clerk who Defected to Canada, Turning over Soviet Secrets

Born outside of Moscow in 1919, Igor Gouzenko, the son of a Czarist sympathiser and school teacher, was educated at Rostov-on-Don and Verkne Spasskoye.

He attended the Moscow Engineering Academy and the Moscow Architectural Institute and joined the Komsomol (the Communist Youth Movement) in 1937. He was recruited by the NKVD in 1939 and served as code and cipher clerk, then as an intelligence officer on the front lines during World War II battles against the German Army in 1941.

He was sent to Ottawa, Canada in 1943, working in the Russian Embassy as a cipher clerk but also spying on Canadian authorities and sending secret information about them back to Moscow.

He was exposed to a free society for the first time and grew to like the Canadian lifestyle. He also grew disenchanted with the Soviet system and when he was unexpectedly recalled to Moscow in 1944, decided to defect. On September 5, 1945 left the Soviet embassy with a briefcase stuffed full of secret documents. These documents exposed the existence of and size and scope of a Soviet spy ring operating within the Canadian borders. He went to a Canadian newspaper in an attempt to turn this information over but was laughed out of the offices and considered a crank. Likewise, attempted to turn his information over to the Canadian governmental authorities, but they also refused to believe his story and returned to the newspaper once again.

Terrified that his theft had been exposed, he and his family hid in their apartment that night, ignoring several loud knocks on the door. He contacted his neighbour, a Canadian Air Force officer and explained his story to him. The officer helped him to hide his family and contacted the Royal Canadian Mounted Police. A few days later, four men crashed through the door of Gouzenko's apartment and ransacked it. The men were detained by the police who identified them as employees of the Soviet Embassy. When an inspector on the scene turned his head, the four men fled.

On September 8, 1945, the Soviet Embassy complained about their employees being detained and questioned, citing their diplomatic immunity. Embassy officials demanded that Gouzenko, whom they described as a criminal, be arrested and turned over to them. They claimed that he had stolen funds from the Embassy and wanted to return him to Moscow for prosecution.

Gouzenko was in the custody of the Royal Mounted Canadian Police and had provided them with a number of documents, the quality of which were compelling enough for them to realise that he was genuine about his desire to defect. The papers described a world-wide spy operation, set into place by the Soviet Union and operating throughout the world. Under protective custody, Gouzenko continued to expound upon his claims. He exposed numerous Soviet agents (listed on index cards from the Embassy) and provided them with notes from the casebook of Soviet spymaster Colonel Nicolai Zabotin. Canadian officials quickly thereafter shared these revelations with the U.S. and British governments.

Because he was exposed by Gouzenko, Colonel Zabotin was recalled to Moscow and was sentenced to four years of hard labour for allowing a disgruntled employee to compromise the entire Soviet spy apparatus. He appeared several times on Canadian television wearing a hood over his head in order to conceal his identity. Gouzenko penned his autobiography titled "This was My Choice" in 1948.

Gouzenko died in 1982.

Christine Granville

Polish-born British SOE Known for her Daring Exploits in Intelligence and Sabotage Missions

Krystyna Skarbek was born in Warsaw, Poland in 1915. She was the daughter of Count Jerzy Skarbek, a Polish aristocrat and the granddaughter of a wealthy Jewish banker in the Goldfeder family. She was educated in a convent in Warsaw and at the age of 17 was crowned Miss Poland after winning a beauty contest.

She was married briefly but divorced her husband soon thereafter. She remarried, this time to Georg Gizycki, a writer who was twice her age. After they were married, they were living in Africa, where he was working on a book, when Nazi Germany invaded Poland in 1939. The couple immediately travelled to Britain and she volunteered to work with British intelligence services (her husband joined the Free Polish Services and was later killed in combat).

Krystyna was brought into the Special Operations Executive branch of British intelligence, recruited because of her intellect and her fluency in several languages. She was given the name Christine Granville by SOE and used it for the rest of her life.

She was to work with resistance group in fighting the Nazi invasion and received special training in espionage.

She was assigned to Budapest where she worked under the cover of a journalist. Her real purpose was to aid Polish refugees to escape across the border. An excellent skier, she skied several times across the Tatra Mountains into Poland to retrieve escaped Polish prisoners of war and bring them out of the country. She would go on to establish several escape routes, bringing Polish refugees back into England.

She was sent to parachute training in Cairo, Egypt and would use this training for numerous jumps into Nazi-occupied France. She was also assigned to gather information on German troop readiness in Poland as well as information on German armaments, including a new anti-tank gun. She travelled several times between England and Poland delivering this information. On her trip into Poland, she was stopped by German soldiers. She reportedly pulled the pins out of two live grenades and told the soldiers that if they attempted to take her into custody, she would drop the grenades, killing all of them. The soldiers allowed her to retreat to safety.

She was stopped on another trip at the border but dumped incriminating evidence into a river beforehand. Unfortunately, she was still in possession of a large sum of money which she could not explain. Brazenly, she told the guards to either take the money and let her and her comrades go or to turn everything over to their superiors (who would keep the money). The guards kept the money and let them escape. On another occasion, when stopped by border guards, she convinced them that she and her companions were simple farm peasants on their way to have a picnic. On yet another occasion where she and her companions were arrested by Hungarian police, she bluffed her way out of trouble, convincing them that she was related to Admiral

Horthy, Regent of Hungary. She was soon thereafter released and made her way back to England with photos showing German troop buildup.

She was parachuted into southern France in 1944 and was used as a courier, using the name Pauline (and sometimes Jacqueline) Armand, delivering messages and materials that could not be transmitted via radio or telegraph to Cairo.

Granville was often used to spread propaganda, insisting that England would not abandon Poland in its fight against Nazi Germany and convincing Italian troops to desert their German allies. She worked for a period of time under Colonel Francois Cammaerts, head of the 10,000 troop maquis in Rhone Valley. When he and two allies were captured in Digne and imprisoned as spies, Granville reportedly met with the Nazi commandant and convinced him that if he did not release the three men immediately, he would be shot by the approaching Allied forces (A more likely scenario is that she claimed to be the niece of British General Montgomery, and threatened two local Digne liaisons. They demanded that she write out a statement clearing them of collaborating with the Nazi and also demanding monetary payment, both of which were accommodated).

As soon as the war ended, Granville was released from her intelligence duties and was forced to find any work she could. She worked for a time as switchboard operator at the India Hotel in London, then as a saleswoman at Harrod's department store and later an attendant at the Paddington hotel.

In 1951, she took a job as a stewardess on the ocean liner, Winchester Castle which sailed between England, Australia and South Africa. Her superior on the liner was a steward named Dennis Muldowney. Muldowney who suffered from schizophrenia became obsessed with Granville and declared his love for her. After she rebuffed his advance several times,

Granville quit her job and moved to London. Muldowney followed her there, quitting his job and taking a position with the Reform Club in Winchester. Again professing his love for her, Muldowney was told by Granville in no uncertain terms that she wanted him to leave her alone. After this final rejection, Muldowney, began stalking her. On June 15, 1952, Muldowney spotted her walking down the stairs in her hotel and rushing to her, stabbed her to death. Muldowney was sentenced to death for the murder and was hanged in September 1952 at Pentonville Prison.

Granville was buried with the French Croix de Guerre, a medal from Poland, the George Medal for Special Services, the Order of the British Empire and the badge of the French Resistance.

Theodore Alvin Hall

American Physicist and an Atomic Spy for the Soviet Union

Born in 1926, Theodore Alvin Hall, the son of a furrier, grew into a tall, handsome youngman with a pleasing personality.

A Graduate of Harvard University he was a star physicist. He served in the United States Army during World War II but had leftist beliefs early on, feeling that the Soviet philosophy was more ideologically align with his views. He met Saville "Savy" Sax while attending Harvard, the two sharing common socio-political beliefs.

He was assigned to work on the Manhattan Project in Los Alamos, New Mexico, helping to develop the atomic bomb. He believed that the United States unilateral control over Atomic bomb weaponry gave the country too much power that could lead to possible disaster if there was no other country with the proper tools to serve as a counter-balance. He decided to help to even the balance of power by providing information to the Soviet Union in order to aid them in their own Atomic research. Along with Sax, he made contact with Soviet officials to initiate an information transfer.

Sax made contact with Nicola Napoli, the president of Soviet cultural propaganda organisation in New York City called Artkino. Sax told Napoli that he had a friend who was privy to top secret atomic research information and wanted to share it with the Soviet Union. Hall, at the same time visited the Amtorg, an import/export company that served as a cover for the base of operations for a network of Soviet spies. There he spoke with a warehouse worker who directed him to meet with Sergei Kurnakov, a Soviet journalist based in New York. Napoli had also suggested that Sax meet with Kurnakov.

Hall was scheduled to return to Los Alamos a few days later, so Kurnakov was pressed to make a determination whether Sax and Hall were legitimate in their offer or were undercover agents for the FBI. The decision was made that two potential for gaining valuable information far exceeded the accompanying risks.

Moscow received a cable on November 12, 1944, detailing the offer by the young spies. Hall was given the code name "Mlas" which meant young and Sax, a year older than Hall was referred to as "Star" meaning old. Hall obtained and Sax delivered numerous documents and design pals for atomic weapons research including information about implosion experiments to the Soviets.

The United States learned of Hall's espionage activity when it deciphered intercept Soviet cable messages. These messages, known as the Venona documents provided clear evidence of Hall and Sax. However, the United States, unwilling to alert the Soviets to the fact that they had broken the Soviets code, confronted Hall but did not pursue legal action against him. Hall went on to become a noted biophysicist at Cambridge University, working with biological X-ray research.

In 1996, the Venona documents were made public by the NSA. Hall, in ill health with cancer and Parkinson's disease, acknowledged that he may have been wrong about the Soviet government, but refused to apologise for his actions. Hall died in 1999.

Robert Hanssen

American FBI Agent who Passed Information to Soviet Intelligence

Robert Hanseen was born on April 18, 1944 in Chicago, Illinois.

He was the son of a Chicago police officer and a housewife, Howard Hansen who was part of a special division called the Red Unit, created to ferret out communist sympathisers during the Red Scare.

Robert Hanssen attended Knox College in Galeswood, Illinois, majoring in Chemistry while also taking Russian as a foreign language. After being rejected for a position as a cryptographer with the NSA, enrolled in the Dental School of Northwestern University in 1966. At Northwestern, Hanssen became known for his penchant for wearing Black suits to class every day. In 1968, halfway through the Dental program,

Hanssen grew tired of it and decided he would rather become a psychiatrist. After growing tired of this pursuit, he returned to Northwestern and earned an MBA in accounting and information systems.

He met Bonnie Wauck, a student nurse at a state mental facility in Chicago in 1965. The two married on August 10, 1968. Wauck was the daughter of a University professor and a practicing Catholic, and member of the Opus Dei organisation. Four years later, Robert enrolled in the Chicago Police Department and was soon assigned to a special training class for a new division of the department that focused on police corruption.

He was distrusted by many within the division, including his boss, John Clarke. He was considered a devoted family man in his community, spending time with his children, teaching them to excel at academics. He also became an enthusiastic member of Opus Dei, which was deemed a cult by many. The organisation instructed its members to attend Catholic church services every day and confession once each week. He applied twice to the FBI and was accepted the second time in January 1976, and was assigned to the Bureau's Gary, Indiana office but was transferred two years later to New York City. Living with his wife and four children in Scarsdale, New York, Hanssen was having a tough time making ends meet and decided to exploit his position with the FBI.

Disenchanted by the lackadaisical attitude of fellow FBI agents, Hanssen approached Russian agents and offered to sell secret documents. He was rewarded famously for his efforts but was caught by his wife while counting $20,000 and writing a letter to the Soviets in his basement. Thinking he was writing a love letter to a girlfriend, she demanded to know what was going on. He admitted to her where he had gotten the money but claimed that he had only given the Soviets useless information. Instead, he had actually provided the Soviets with very valuable information, including the identity of Dmitri Polyakov, a top-level Soviet double agent. In place of turning him to the authorities, she convinced him to confess his actions to an Opus Dei priest. The priest instructed him to give up his activities and to donate the money, he received, to Mother Teresa's charities.

He was considered a highly intelligent agent, but his tepid interpersonal skill as well as his continued preference for black suits caused many to tag him with the nickname "the Mortician".

Unfortunately, the perception that he was an aloof, introverted worker hindered his upward mobility within the Bureau. He was transferred to the FBI headquarters in Washington, DC where he was initially assigned to develop a budget for the Bureau that was to be presented to the Congress. He was moved to the Soviet Analytical Unit in 1983 and given a high security clearance. After a four year stint, he was called back to New York.

He decided to re-establish his link to the Soviets. Knowing that the FBI was not conducting surveillance on Victor Degtyar, a KGB Colonel living in Alexandria, Virginia, Hanssen sent a letter to Degtyar, with instructions to pass another letter on to Victor Cherkashin, the head of Soviet espionage efforts in Washington. In this letter, Hanssen offered to turn over classified and highly sensitive information to the Soviets in return for $100,000. He also provided the name of three Russian agents who were working for the United States. Two of the agents were executed and one was imprisoned.

He dropped off some documents at a dead drop and was rewarded with a payment of $50,000. For the next six years, Hanssen continued to deliver classified information to his Soviet contacts, many involving nuclear weaponry and satellite information. One of his secrets passed included the inner workings of the COINS-II (Community On-Line Intelligence System). He provided Soviets with extraordinary logistical information, including information related to U.S. readiness in the event of a nuclear war. Over this period of time, he collected more than $ 600,000 for his services as well as the acknowledgement of his importance. His information was directed to the Soviet heads in Moscow and he received official letters of praise of the director of the KGB. He was also promised that $100,000 had been deposited for him in an interest bearing account in a Soviet bank. Hanssen never told the Russian agents his real name, although he did, on occasion, use the alias Ramon Garcia.

In 1990, Mark Wauck, Bonnie's brother and also an FBI agent, learned that Bob had stashed away thousands of dollars in cash and spent money more freely than he had previously been doing. Mark suspected that Bob might be engaged in spying and reported his suspicions to FBI officials in Chicago. These warnings, however, went unheeded and were ignored.

While betraying his country as a spy, Hanssen seemed to become even more committed in his devotion to the Opus Dei organisation, attending meetings and rallys fervently and sending his children to Opus Dei schools. He often seemed obsessed with religious and moral issues such as abortion. Despite these high principles, he engaged in lurid activities. He interacted online with pornographic internet websites and chat rooms. He was reported to have filmed himself having sex with his wife and watched the tape with a friend. Most bizarre, however, was a relationship he developed with a stripper named Priscilla Galey.

Hanssen gave her money and jewellery and even provided for extensive dental work for her. He also took her on trips abroad and purchased a Mercedes-Benz for her. Surprisingly, however, despite lavishing her with such expensive gifts, Hanssen never pursued a sexual relationship with her. He seemed more intent on changing her life and leading her to religion. The relationship ended when she became involved in drugs. He was accused of making advances towards women in the FBI office and was suspended once for pushing an administrative assistant to the ground and was disciplined for his actions.

In 1991, following the fall of the Soviet Union, Hanssen felt that the instability of the nation (and its intelligence community and operatives) made it too dangerous to continue in his espionage activities. For the next eight years, he continued on at the FBI, but when former KGB official Vladimir Putin rose to power in 1999, Hanssen felt it was time to get back into the game and he re-established contact with the Russians.

In September 2000, a Russian agent cooperating with the FBI provided files he had received and included the plastic bags in which they were delivered. Robert Hanssen's fingerprints were found on these bags. The FBI quietly began surveillance on him and videotaped him taking documents marked SECRET from the FBI office. The Bureau went so far as to bug his home, office and car and purchased a house across the street from where they increased their surveillance.

He was observed making numerous trips to Foxstone Park where Hanssen checked for a signal that the Russians were ready to trade information for money.

On February 18, 2001, Hanssen went to church and then dropped off his friend Jack Hoschuer at Dulles Airport in Virginia. He traveled to Foxstone Park, near his Vienna, Virginia home, got out of his car and walked over to a footbridge, under which he left of package. The package contained the documents he had taken from his office and a computer diskette upon which was a goodbye letter to his Russian "friends".

The letter stated:

Dear Friends,

I thank you for your assistance these many years. It seems, however, that my greatest utility to you has come to an end, and it is time to seclude myself from active service... Life is full of its ups and downs... I will be in contact next year, same time same place.

As he made the "dead drop", 10 FBI agents converged upon him, placing him under arrest. Hanssen was said to have exclaimed "What took you so long?" Bonnie Hanssen was taken into custody and interrogated but claimed she didn't believe her husband was a spy.

The Justice Department wanted to pursue the death penalty for the man they called the most damaging FBI turncoat in history.

Instead, in June 2001, Hanssen was able to cut a deal, receiving life in prison without the possibility of parole in return for providing full details of his actions. He claimed that he spied against his country in order to provide for his family and because of his resentment for being passed over for job promotions. He showed little remorse for his action and was sentenced on May 10, 2002 and assigned to the Federal prison in Lewisburg, Pennsylvania.

❖❖❖

Mata Hari

A Dutch Exotic Dancer who Worked as a Double Agent for France and Germany

Mata Hari was born as Margaret Gertrude Zelle on August 7, 1876 in Leeuwarden, Holland to father Adam Zelle, a Dutch hatter and his Japanese wife Antje van der Meulen. The family was very wealthy and well to do and raised her in a very happy home with a comfortable lifestyle. After her mother's death in 1890, she was sent by her father to live in a convent. Briefly attending a teaching school but was expelled after allegedly having sex with the school's headmaster.

In 1894, she answered a "lonely hearts club" advertisement placed by John Rudolph MacLeod, a Dutch colonial officer in the Dutch East Indies, who was 20 years her senior.

The couple married in 1895 and moved to Java where they lived until 1901. The couple's early years were anything but ideal as she engaged in scandalous affairs and he often slept with other women in their house while she was in the next room.

The couple had a son named Norman in January

1896, but the child died, believed to have been poisoned by a former house servant with a vendetta against John. They also had another child, a daughter named Jeanne. At this time, it is rumoured, the couple engaged in a blackmail scheme by which Margaret would entice a wealthy landowner into her bed, whereupon John would storm angrily into the room, threatening the man with scandal and then blackmailing him for a lucrative sum (some of the details were revealed during the couple's divorce proceedings). Despite their money schemes, the marriage was filled with quarrels and John physically abused her. The couple divorced sometime between 1902 and 1904.

With custody of her daughter, Margaret struggled financially, especially after her husband stopped sending support payments. What money she did have she used on dancing lessons, learning the Oriental dances she had seen in Java. After sending her daughter to live with relatives, she embarked upon her new career, performing the mysterious dances of the God Shiva. Her early efforts were unsuccessful, as she was unable to secure bookings and was alleged to have worked as a prostitute for a period of time.

When World War I broke out, Mata Hari had decided to engage in another exciting profession – espionage. Having already engaged in numerous affairs with numerous wealthy men and many important people in the military and intelligence community as her paramours.

The Chief of the Berlin Police Department, Traugott von Jagow was one of them and he suggested to her that she include pillow talk in her meeting with her important clients, obtaining secrets as well as money from them. She was given the German code number H.21, which would prove significant years later.

Travelled throughout Europe, attending embassy functions and social occasions, meeting military and political contacts. After seducing, the men, she would pry information about troops and weaponry as well as political alliances and military tactics. She reported this information back to Jagow and was positioning herself neatly when the War began.

Having been granted German citizenship, she was ordered to make her way into France where she began passing secrets to the Germans. Although French agents kept her under surveillance, they were unable to collect sufficient evidence against her to arrest her. Much of her information, at this point, was vital, helping to prepare the Germans develop their strategy to overpower the French troops.

French counterintelligence officers finally grew wise to her and she was confronted by Captain Georges Ladoux. Ladoux informed her that he was going to have her deported back to Holland, whereupon she shocked him by proposing to spy on behalf of France and against Germany. Bragging that she had access to high level German intelligence, she offered that she could make it available to France. In so offering this aid, she destroyed her original alibi that she was not involved in espionage nor privy to any intelligence. Ladoux, pretended to take her up on her offer and sent her off to Brussels with the names of six French agent with whom she could make contact. Almost immediately thereafter, Ladoux received information from the British that one of the six agents had been arrested by the Germans, which convinced him that she was a considerable security risk and ordered her arrest immediately.

German intelligence had come to find that Mata Hari had been identified and therefore compromised. She was therefore of little use to them. After offering her services to other foreign nations, she boldly demanded from Jagow that she be paid in full for her espionage activities. Jagow ordered her to return to France where she would be paid. French authorities arrested her on February 13, 1917 and took her to the Fauborg Saint-Denis prison.

Mata Hari was tried for espionage in July 1917, represented by one of the top attorneys in France. Although much of the evidence against her was weak, French authorities were able to show that the payment she returned to France to collect was designated for German agent H.21. The "H" signified that she was an agent for Germany before World War I started. She argued that the payment was for her sexual services and not for espionage. The jury was unmoved, quickly returning a guilty verdict and sentenced her to death. On October 15, 1917 a calm Mata Hari faced a firing squad and was executed.

Historians believe that Mata Hari, despite her notoriety and name, was rather incompetent and ineffective spy, caught up in the excitement of her own fascination. Most believe, as did much of the intelligence community of her time, that she was in way over her head and did not realise the ramifications of her duplicitous activities, naively believing that she could charm her way out of any situation. In later years, however, Mata Hari has gained many supporters. In 1932, the French government admitted that the evidence and therefore the case against her was negligible at best while the German government labelled her contributions to its war efforts as insubstantial.

Alger Hiss

U.S. State Department Official Accused of Espionage

Born in Baltimore, Maryland in 1904, Alger Hiss lost his father early as he committed suicide when he was only three years old.

Hiss attended the prestigious Johns Hopkins University from which he graduated in 1926. He moved on to Harvard University Law School and after graduation in 1929 served as a law clerk for the esteemed United States Supreme Court Justice Oliver Wendell Holmes and then practiced law in New York and Massachusetts. In 1929, he married Priscilla Fansler Hobson. Four year later he moved to Washington, D.C. in 1933 where he worked for the Roosevelt administration in the Agricultural Adjustment Administration until 1935. Next, he moved to the Department of Justice where he worked until 1936 and then to the State Department in 1936. He served as Secretary to the Nye Commission on Munitions as well as Assistant General Counsel to the Solicitor General of the United States.

At the State Department, he was a very important figure, travelling with President Franklin Roosevelt to the Yalta Conference where Roosevelt met to discuss allied strategies for World War II. He served as a top aide to Secretary of State Edward Stettinius.

Later on, he served as the Secretary General for the Dumbarton Oaks Conference in which the United Nations was established. In 1946, he was named President of the Carnegie Endowment for International Peace and worked in that capacity until 1948.

In 1948, Whitaker Chambers, the Senior Editor for Time Magazine and a former member of the Communist Party went before the House Un-American Activities Committee and testified that Hiss was a Communist and had passed classified State Department documents to Soviet agents.

Hiss denied the charges and offered to testify before the committee. In his testimony, he vehemently denied that he was a Communist and stated that he had never even met Whitaker Chambers. Chambers responded by supplying detailed recollections of Hiss and his family with an uncanny accuracy. Hiss corroborated many of these recollections and explained that he may have known Chambers years earlier under a different name and in a different appearance. The highly regarded Hiss was now being viewed with some suspicion.

Chambers made an appearance on the American political television show "Meet the Press". When he was asked about Hiss, Chambers repeated the statement he had made before the committee. Hiss immediately sued Chambers for slander. Chambers continued to provide evidence against Hiss, by providing photographs of documents that appeared to be re-typed copies of State Department documents which also included some notes in Hiss' handwriting.

Chambers further produced undeveloped film which he had hidden in a hollowed out pumpkin on his Maryland farm. The film contained photographs of more classified State Department documents which were later on referred to as the "Pumpkin Papers". The Justice Department was also working with information provided by a Soviet defector named Igor Gouzenko in 1945. Gouzenko had claimed that an assistant to the Secretary of State was a Soviet spy. The FBI had narrowed its search down to Hiss but did not have enough evidence to confront Hiss. The FBI was able to find the typewriter that was alleged to have been used to retype the classified documents.

Hiss was indicted for committing perjury. The trial ended in a hung jury but the second trial in on January 21, 1950 adjudged Hiss as guilty of perjury (note, Hiss was never found guilty of espionage).

He was sentenced to five years in prison and after his subsequent appeal and request for a new trial were denied, he spent four and a half years in the Federal Penitentiary in Lewisburg, Pennsylvania.

The case became a cause celeb, debated across political lines with conservatives believing that Hiss was indeed guilty while liberals felt he was set up with circumstantial and shoddy evidence. Hiss maintained his innocence and spent the rest of his life trying to prove it. In 1996, however, the Venona messages were released, one of which described an assistant to the Secretary of State in 1945 who attended the Yalta Conference but was actually a Soviet spy. Sources at the National Security Agency have stated that this could refer only to Hiss.

Hiss died in 1996.

Roger Hollis

Director General of M15 who was Later Accused of being a Soviet Agent

The son of a Bishop of a Church in England, Roger Hollis was born in 1905.

He attended Oxford University where he befriended a fellow student named Claud Cockburn but left the school without graduating. He obtained a job with the British American Tobacco Company and was sent to Shanghai. While in Shanghai, it is believed that he came in contact with Richard Sorge, a top Soviet spy as well as Communist agents Agnes Smedley and Ruth Kuczynski (Kuczynski developed several Soviet spy rings in Europe and the Far East).

He developed a case of tuberculosis in 1934 and travelled to Switzerland for medical treatment, passing through Moscow first by way of the Trans-Siberian railroad. After being cured, returned to England and sought employment with the SIS in 1938. Although he was rejected due to his poor health, he joined MI5 in 1939. Within MI5, he worked with the Branch that focused on the Communist Party and the Soviet Union. Later on, he helped to set up the Australian Security and Intelligence Organisation and then served as the head of MI5's C division that handled internal security issues.

He was sent to Canada in 1945 for his first important mission. He was to debrief Igor Gouzenko, a former cipher clerk within the Russian Embassy in Ottawa, Canada who had defected to the West (MI6 officer Kim Philby should have handled the matter but was busy trying hush up another Soviet defector). He was told by Gouzenko of a major Soviet penetration of MI5 and specifically about the existence of a high level mole within (codenamed "Elli"). Hollis failed to report Gouzenko's allegations.

Was promoted to the position of Deputy Director of MI5 in 1953 and then became the Director in 1956.

In 1961, KGB defector Anatoli Golitsyn described an elaborate spy ring within Britain, naming Guy Burgess and Donald MacLean as members of the "Ring of Five". As MI5 began to close in on Philby, who it was thought, was another member of the ring, he was tipped off about his impending arrest and fled to Moscow in 1963. Hollis was one of only five senior-level MI5 officers who knew that Philby was to be arrested and it is believed that he tipped off his friend.

In 1963, he failed to provide British Prime Minister Harold MacMillan information concerning Russian spy Yevgeny Ivanov, who was involved in the Profumo scandal that rocked England and eventually forced MacMillan to resign from his position. In 1964, he approved of the deal in which Anthony Blunt, the fourth member of the Ring of Five, received immunity from prosecution. He was knighted by Queen Elizabeth and resigned in 1965.

He was the subject of intense speculation based on numerous close, personal friendships and contacts with known and exposed spies as well as his less than stellar tenure and the Director-General. Hollis was referred to quietly as Mr. Inertia because of his lethargy in taking action.

He was brought into MI5 offices and questioned at length by intelligence officer Peter Wright and Sir Martin Jones, the man who replaced him as Director-General. Hollis denied being involved in any espionage activities against Britain and the matter was closed. Still, several books have boldly stated the likelihood that Hollis was indeed the Fifth Man.

After his resignation, he was divorced by his wife of more than 30 years and married his long-time secretary.

Hollis Died in 1973.

❖❖❖

Noor Inayat Khan

British SOE Agent who Worked with the French Resistance

Born on January 1, 1914 in Russia, the daughter of an Indian father and an American mother, Noor Inayat Khan gained fames while she was yet a teenager. Her father was assigned to spread Sufi (a sect of Indian Muslim) philosophy and his travels took him to Russia where he became friends with the writer Leo Tolstoy and the mystic Rasputin. The family moved to London in 1917 and then settled in France in 1920.

After the death of her father in 1921, Inayat began attending school, eventually entering the Sorbonne where she studied juvenile psychology. Unfortunately, she suffered a nervous breakdown at this time. She returned to academics entering Ecole de Langues Orientales at the University of Paris in 1937.

She began writing for children soon after, first for radio broadcast and then for a children's newspaper she founded. It was called Bel Age. Upon the German invasion of France in 1940 she fled to England with her family. Her brother joined the Royal Navy and she became a member of the Women's Auxiliary Air Force.

She entered the Special Operations Executive (SOE) and was trained as a radio operator. She was inserted into France to work with the French underground using the codename "Madeline" and radioed information to the allies regarding resistance activities as well as providing intelligence for allied operations.

Working under the name Jeanne-Marie Regnier, she rode her bicycle to the National School of Agriculture at Grignon (which served as her spy network's headquarters) everyday, delivering messages from London and receiving new messages to send back to London.

On July 1, 1943, Noor arrived at the headquarters late, only to see almost a hundred SS and Gestapo agents entering the building. She watched helplessly as they led her fellow comrades from the facility and took them into custody. Returning to Paris she reported what she had witnessed but it was too late to fully warn her superiors as additional raids occurred. Most of the top SOE officials and resistance workers had been captured and were now in custody.

Because she had become a key figure in the SOE work, Maurice Buckmaster, the Chief of SOE operations feared for Noor's life and ordered her back to England. Noor refused, staying on in France, determined to continue acting as a much needed radio operator. For the next three months, Inayat Khan moved from location to location, transmitting messages late in the night to avoid detection.

Her courage and quick thinking helped her to get out of predicaments several times but eventually she was betrayed by a French woman who reported her activity to the Gestapo for 500 pounds. She was caught in the act by Gestapo agents as she tried to send a message to London. She was taken into custody and immediately escaped through a window, trying to move from rooftop to rooftop but was recaptured.

Noor was subjected to extreme interrogation but refused to talk and bravely requested to be shot immediately. When the Gestapo confined her to a room in its headquarters, she collaborated with to other prisoners and escaped from the facility. Just as they were making their getaway from the compound, air raids sirens caused German officers to conduct a security check, exposing Noor and her compatriots and prompting their recapture.

Inayat Khan was transferred to Pforzheim Prison in Germany where she was kept manacled to the wall in order to prevent further escape attempts. She was later transferred to Dachau and was ordered to be executed by SS Chief Heinrich Himmler. She was executed on September 12, 1944 along with three other women and was posthumously awarded the George Cross by the French government.

Vernon Kell

First Director General of the British Security Service (M15)

Born on November 21, 1873 in Yarmouth, England, Kell was the son of a wealthy family, provided with advanced training, speaking Polish and English at an early age. He graduated from the Royal Military Academy in Sandhurst in 1892, fluent in several languages including French, German and Italian in addition to the Polish and English.

He served in the British military and was sent to Moscow where he quickly learned Russian. He returned to England where he married Constance Scott on April 5, 1900. Immediately thereafter, he was sent to China where he fought to put down the Boxer Rebellion.

He returned to London and was transferred to the War Offices' German Desk and was placed on the Committee of Imperial Defense in 1907. He was named director of MO5 (Military Operation 5), the newly developed counterespionage department in 1909. In 1916, the name of the agency was changed to MI5. He worked alongside of and asked advice from many of the top military and security experts in Britain.

He initiated a purge of spies from throughout England. Kell ordered that the purge take place all at once in order to prevent any from escaping due to being tipped off. Many of the top spies in the country were gathered up in the purge. Later Kell would authorise the hunt for Karl Lody, the top German spy in London.

He enjoyed a heralded career during World War I and into the 1930's, being promoted all the way to the rank of Major-General. He was considered one of the top counterespionage experts in the world, both for his methods of investigation and for his knowledge of the subject.

He had an acrimonious relationship with Winston Churchill, Britain's Prime Minister during World War II. Speculation was that Churchill held a grudge against Kell for not sharing classified information with him in the 1920's, a period where Churchill was not in power.

On October 14, 1939, a German submarine sent a torpedo into the side of the British battleship, the Royal Oak. When the ship sank, 834 men died. Later, in 1940, an explosion occurred in the Royal Gunpowder Factory in Waltham Abbey. Both incidents were initially considered to have been the result of espionage and sabotage undetected by Kell's MI5. Although later investigations tended to prove that this was not the case, Churchill jumped at the opportunity to cast a dark shadow on Kell. On May 25, 1940, Churchill fired Vernon Kell, removing him from his position as the head of MI5.

Crushed shocked and devastated by his dismissal, Kell, having dedicated his life to serving his country was heartbroken and retired to a small cottage in Buckinghamshire where he died on March 27, 1942.

Ruth Kuczynski

German-born Soviet Spy who Operated a Spy Ring in China

Ruth was born in Berlin, Germany in 1907, the daughter of German-Jewish professor and Soviet spy Rene Kuczynski. Her brother Jurgen and sister Bridgitte also became Soviet spies.

She became a Communist in 1924 when she became a member of the Communist Youth Movement. She was selected to be the head of the German Communist Party's Propaganda Section.

Ruth moved to the United States with her father and brother who were engaged in espionage activities for the GRU. She returned to Germany in 1929 and married Rudolph Hamburger, a friend from her childhood.

In 1930, she was instructed by Soviet Intelligence to move to Shanghai, China. Her husband, also a Soviet spy was already in Shanghai, under the guise of an architect. Ruth was more important to the GRU than her husband as she operated a major spy ring in China.

She became close friends with Agnes Smedley, an American journalist who would ultimately introduce Kuczynski to Soviet agent Richard Sorge. Ruth began an affair with Sorge. She often allowed him to use her apartment as a meeting place. She established a cover as a journalist writing for pro-Communist newspapers.

She was ordered back to Moscow for advanced training in 1933, but returned to China six months later, under a new cover as a bookseller. Her actual task was to develop a strong relationship between the GRU and Chinese Communists in Manchuria who were fighting against the Japanese.

She worked with a GRU whom she knew only as Ernst. It is believed that she engaged in an affair with him and gave birth to a daughter in 1935. Her daughter was believed to be Ernst's child.

She was sent to Peking (now Beijing) in 1935. Chinese intelligence, with the help of Morris "Two Gun" Cohen, did a sweep of suspected spies, arresting Sorge's replacement. Ruth and her husband escaped with her two daughters. They returned to London and visited her parents (her father was now teaching economics at the London School of Economics).

She was joined in England by Olga "Ollo" Muth, her former nanny from Germany. Muth became a nanny for Ruth's newborn daughter Nina. Muth, at this point, was unaware of the couple's espionage activities. She accompanied her husband to Poland where Rudolph would serve as Senior GRU officer.

Ruth was ordered back to Moscow for further training in June 1937. She was also awarded the Order of the Red Banner by the Soviet Union for her espionage activities and then order to Switzerland in 1938 to establish a new spy ring. She stopped first in England to meet with prospective agents, one of whom was Alexander Foote. Foote was further assessed by Brigitte Kuczynski. Foote joined her in Montreuz, Switzerland in 1938 to serve as a radio operator. Moving in with her, he began operating under the code-name "Sonia". Merged her burgeoning network with the Lucy spy ring operated by Alexander Rado. She welcomed a new member into her spy ring named Leon Beurton, and started a relationship with Beurton immediately, ending the one with Foote.

She started denouncing the Soviet Union and the principles of Communism after Russia signed a non-aggression pact with Nazi Germany in 1939. She was actually acting on orders from the GRU in order to develop a guise for a deep cover operation planned for her. The GRU wanted to her to live as a British citizen, and thus requested that she marry Foote. Instead she married Beurton in February 1940 (she divorced Hamburger in late 1939). She obtained a British passport soon thereafter and prepared to move to England.

She did not plan to take Ollo with them to England. Ollo, distraught over the prospect of being separated from the children and angry at Sonia and Beurton, informed British authorities of their espionage activities but no one took much note of her claims and failed to follow up on them.

She moved to Liverpool, England in February 1941 and then to Oxford and prepared for her new espionage activities. She was joined by Beurton in the summer of 1942 but he was soon drafted into the British Army. She was assigned to oversee the activities of Klaus Fuchs, the atomic bomb researcher who had provided so much information during his work on the Manhattan project. Fuchs had originally been recruited into the Communist party by Brigitte Kuczynski. Her father had provided aide to her at several points during her activities, as had her brother, who would eventually be made a Lieutenant Colonel in the United States Army and in a great position to pass information to her.

She was placed under suspicion when her contacts with Fuchs came to light after his arrest. She was also linked to Sir Roger Hollis, former head of MI5, with whom Sonia had become acquainted in Switzerland and China. Speculation held that Sonia had actually recruited Hollis into Soviet control but he vehemently denied even knowing her. She was questioned along with her husband by British agents in 1947 regarding their alleged involvement in espionage activities. Both refused to answer any questions and no further investigation was evident.

She fled to East Germany with her children in 1950 and was joined by Beurton one year later. She received her second Order of the Red Banner award in 1969 as well as the Order of Karl Marx in 1984. She wrote several books including her autobiography in 1977. She was considered by many to be the greatest female spy ever.

❖❖❖

Carl Lody

German Soldier who Spied on England during World War I

Born in 1879 in Berlin, Germany, Carl Lody served in the German Navy, rising to the rank of lieutenant before retiring. He took a job as guide on a Hamburg-America ocean liner, taking the rich on cruises around the world. He left the cruise at the brink of World War I, moved to Berlin and volunteered for service in the German Navy but was sent to German Naval Intelligence, because of his ability to speak English. He was sent to England to spy on the British fleet and provide an assessment of its size and battle-worthiness. Lody was promised that this mission would be a one-time event, after which he was free to return to his job on the cruise lines, having fully satisfied his duty to his country. He was trained in espionage and sent to Norway under the name "Charles Inglis". He continued on to Scotland in 1914 and monitored the British fleet there, counting the number of warships and estimating their military value.

Because of poor training, he failed to take the most simple precautions to conceal his intentions and was therefore monitored by British MI5 agents. His mail was intercepted and he was followed by for almost a week before he realised it, at which point he immediately fled Scotland and returned to London,

England. In London, he once again made blunders in seeking information. He approached people at military installations and bluntly asked them questions that would unquestionably draw suspicions. Having drawn an inordinate amount of attention to himself while scouting out British military installations, Lody moved on again, returning to Scotland.

Travelling around the British territories, he continued gathering information, sketching buildings and machinery and assessing troop readiness. Eventually he returned to England, whereupon he was arrested and court-martialed. Confined in the Tower of London, he was found guilty of spying and sentenced to death. On November 6, Lody was executed by a firing squad at the Tower of London.

Clayton Lonetree

A United States Marine Coerced into Passing Secrets to the Soviet Union

Born in 1961 in St. Paul, Minnesota, Clayton Lonetree was the grandson of the Chief of the Winnebago Native American tribe.

He was enlisted in the United States Marine Corps in 1980 and entered the Marine Corps Security Battalion Guard school, a rigorous, elite training program in which he was instructed in espionage and counterespionage techniques. He was given TOP SECRET security clearance and assigned to the U.S. Embassy in Moscow in 1984.

As part of his assignment, he signed a non-fraternisation agreement, thereby promising not to engage in friendships with Soviet citizens and to report any such contacts. Lonetree apparently received undue attention because most citizens of Moscow had never seen a Native American before. Despite such attention he was described as lonely and sombre and was believed to have begun drinking excessively.

He attended the annual Marine ball in November 1985 and was introduced to Violetta Seina, a 25 year old Russian woman who was an embassy employee. The two began dating soon thereafter. He was part of the Marine unit assigned to provide security for the 1985 summit meeting between Soviet premier Mikhail Gorbachev and U.S. President Ronald Reagan.

He was introduced by Violetta to her "Uncle Sasha", who in reality was a KGB intelligence officer (named Aleksiy Yefimov). Sasha recruited Lonetree to become a "friend of the Soviet Union". Lonetree eventually provided Sasha with information about the embassy and the U.S. Ambassador. Sasha also asked him to plant a "bug" in the Embassy but Lonetree allegedly refused to do, instead provided plans for the building.

He was assigned to the U.S. Embassy in Vienna, Austria in March 1986. While in Vienna, Lonetree met with Sasha and provided him with information about embassy employees and with floor plans to the building. In return, he was given $2,500 US. Over time, Lonetree provided TOP SECRET documents as well as a burn bag containing more than 100 documents related to U.S. arms reduction.

On December 12, 1986, Sasha turned Lonetree over to another handler, who promised to aid Lonetree in re-uniting with Violetta. Two days later, however, Lonetree reported his actions to the CIA station chief. He was immediately turned over to the Navy Intelligence Service (NIS) and placed under arrest, charged with espionage.

NIS launched a nine month investigation, during which all of the Marine guards in the Moscow embassy were replaced. NIS also arrested Corporal Arnold Bracy, who signed a confession indicating that he acted as a lookout for Lonetree, while Lonetree secreted KGB operatives into the embassy to plant bugs. Also arrested was Marine staff Sergeant Robert Stufflebeam, who was charged with failing to report fraternisation with Soviet women. The charges against Bracy and Stufflebeam were eventually dropped.

NIS was highly criticised for its over-exuberance with its investigation, accused of blowing things way out of proportion in order to show off having disrupted a spy operation. Lonetree was convicted on multiple counts of turning over classified information, was court-martialled in 1987 and sentenced to 30 years in prison. Because of his cooperation with authorities, his sentence was reduced to 25 years of which he served nine before being released in February 1996.

Gordon Lonsdale

Soviet Intelligence Officer who Headed a Spy Ring in the U.S.

Born Konon Trofimovich Molody in 1922 in Russia, Gordon Lonsdale moved to California in 1929 and lived with an aunt, becoming fluent in English. He returned to Russia nine years later and became involved with Communist organisations. He joined the Soviet Red Navy and saw action during World War II.

He was involved in intelligence activities during and after the war. He was accepted into the KGB and trained as a spy. He took another name Gordon Arnold Lonsdale from a Canadian who had moved to Finland and died. He journeyed to Canada and the United States and then moved to England in 1955, posing as a businessman (rented jukebox equipment), while actually uncovering information about British underwater capabilities.

He developed a relationship with Harry Houghton, a former Naval petty chief, working in the Underwater Weapons Research Establishment in Portland, Dorset. Houghton's girlfriend, Ethel Gee, worked in the records office of the same Underwater Weapons Research Establishment.

Gee was introduced to Lonsdale who claimed to be a naval attaché for the United States interested in naval research information that Ireland was withholding in defiance of a NATO agreement. Gee agreed to provide secrets, bringing home top secret documents for Houghton to photograph and then returning the next Monday before thy could be discovered missing. Houghton and Gee met Lonsdale once a month.

Polish Intelligence defector, Lt. Colonel Michal Golienewski exposed Lonsdale, Houghton and Gee (as well as George Blake), which subsequently led to their arrests (as well as the arrest of Morris and Leona Cohen). The trio was caught with information about the nuclear submarine Dreadnaught, pamphlets and photographs and undeveloped film of classified British documents (January 7, 1961). Lonsdale was convicted of conspiring to pass classified information and was sentenced to 25 years in prison. In 1964, Lonsdale was exchanged by the British for British agent Greville Wynne and travelled back to the Soviet Union where he was hailed as a national hero, writing a KGB sponsored book (with the help of Kim Philby) entitled Spy in 1965. He suffered a heart attack outside his apartment and died in 1970.

❖❖❖

Donald Maclean

British Diplomat who Became a Spy for the Soviet Union

Born in London, England in 1913, Donald Maclean was the son of Sir Donald Maclean, a noted attorney and Scottish politician. Sir Donald served as a member of Parliament and was knighted in 1917.

He was educated at Gresham and then moved on to Cambridge where he counted within his circle of friends, Anthony Blunt, Guy Burgess and Kim Philby. He was influenced greatly by leftist teachings and believed early on in the cause of communism. He was introduced, while at Cambridge, to a Soviet controller who recruited him into the service of the Soviet Union. He was convinced to disassociate himself from active communist party membership and activity so as not to draw undue attention to himself.

He graduated from Cambridge in 1934 and immediately gained a position in the Foreign Service (despite having acknowledged his leftist leaning while in school). Through contacts loyal to his father, Maclean moved his way up though the ranks of the Foreign Service, attaining a level where he had access to classified information. He passed this information to his Soviet handler.

He was assigned to the Foreign Office Central Department, responsible for Germany, Belgium and France and was assigned to an office in Paris in 1938. He met Melinda Marling, the daughter of an American oil executive, while in Paris and the couple married in 1940 but immediately fled the country due to Nazi occupation. After working for the foreign office for nine years, Maclean was appointed the first secretary for the British Embassy in Washington, DC. He also served as the head of chancery on occasion making him privy to even more information as all material delivered to the British ambassador was easily within his reach. After having a child, Melinda moved to the United States, living in New York with her mother. Donald routinely visited New York City on weekends, ostensibly to visit his wife, but also to pass information to his New York based Soviet contact.

He served as Britain's secretary on the Combined Policy Committee, gaining access to classified information about British and American plans regarding atomic energy and nuclear weaponry. He was also given access to information from the United States Atomic Energy Commission. He worked alongside Alger Hiss, a U.S. State Department official regarding plans for the United Nations and discussed U.S. policy on a number of topics, including U.S. Military participation in South Korea.

He continued his trips to New York, unaware that passages in the Venona documents described a Soviet spy who also visited New York at the same time (in July 1946).

The documents were transmitted accidentally with a lower security encryption and included information from transmissions between British Prime Minister Winston Churchill and U.S. President Harry Truman, including specific serial numbers for those transmission. The serial numbers helped to narrow down the number of people who would have had access to the documents. This information, in addition to his constant requests to participate in meetings of the Atomic Energy Commission led the CIA to maintain surveillance on him.

James Angleton, head of the CIA's counterintelligence program, determined that Maclean was indeed a Soviet spy and caused his pass to the Atomic Energy Commission to be revoked. Angleton informed MI5 of his suspicions and Kim Philby was apprised of the situation. Philby warned Soviet officials and they informed Maclean of the situation.

Maclean, a known bi-sexual, was observed in drunken stupors, prowling for homosexual liaisons. His drinking grew to a dangerous level until he was recalled by the British government and returned home in 1948. He was transferred to Cairo, Egypt where he served as chancery for the British Embassy but again suffered from drunken episodes and was again recalled to London in 1950. Nonetheless, in early 1951 he was assigned a new position, this time as head of the American Department of the Foreign Office.

Maclean's drinking became problematic once again as he vociferously denounced the capitalism of the west and espoused the virtues of communism during dinner parties and formal affairs. Word of his behaviour circulated around London and in January 1951, Kim Philby learned more about the information in the Venona documents and worried that he was in impending jeopardy of being arrested. Concerned that telephone calls or cables to London might be intercepted, Philby sought another way to warn Maclean. Guy Burgess, also enjoying a reputation as a drunkard, engaged in sufficient misbehaviour to merit being sent home from the United States where he was serving with the British embassy. Burgess immediately informed Anthony Blunt of Maclean's impending danger and Blunt likewise informed their Soviet handler Yuri Modin.

Modin immediately set into motion an escape plan and three days before Maclean was to be arrested by MI5, Burgess drove him to Southampton where the two climbed aboard a ferry boat, the S.S. Falaise that took them to St. Malo. Eventually, the two made their way to Moscow where they were hailed as heroes to the Soviet people. Maclean was given the rank of KGB Colonel.

He was joined in September by his wife and children. Maclean and Burgess were put on display for the western press by the Soviet government in 1956. Maclean worked hard to adapt to the Soviet culture and was rewarded by the government with salary and accommodations.

He wrote several publications on economics and was published in the Soviet Union and Britain. In 1966, Melinda Maclean began an affair with Kim Philby, Philby having defected in early 1963. She moved in with him two years later but returned to the United States in 1979.

Donald Maclean died of a heart attack on March 6, 1983. His ashes were buried in England months later.

Allan Nunn May

British Physicist who Passed Atomic Secrets to the Soviet Union

Born in 1912, the London native Allan Nunn May attended Trinity College at Cambridge University from which he graduated with a Ph.D. in physics in1933. While a student, he became a member of the Communist Party.

He joined the Tube Alloys Project, helping to perform research on the development of the atomic bomb in 1942. He was sent to Canada to perform further atomic bomb research in Ottawa in 1944. He was approached by representatives of Soviet Colonel Nikolai Zabotin, a military attaché for the Soviet Embassy and an intelligence officer for the GRU.

He visited the Chicago-based atomic research center and met Major-General Leslie Groves, the head of the Manhattan Project. In 1944, he returned several times to Chicago to conduct experiments with atomic piles and would meet several times with top scientists to discuss the design and development of an atomic bomb.

He provided information about the experimental test blasts in New Mexico and then delivered plutonium and uranium samples to Zabotin. In 1945, Igor Gouzenko, a cipher clerk in the Soviet Embassy in Ottawa, defected to the Canadian government. Gouzenko helped to expose spy rings in the United States and Canada. May was placed under surveillance by MI5.

He returned to England in 1946, having arranged with Zabotin to meet with a new Soviet contact at the British Museum in London. He began lecturing in physics at King's College.

He was interviewed by Lt. Col. Leonard Burt, a representative of Scotland Yard. Burt explained that the interview was simply routine, but then stunned May by informing him that MI5 was aware that he had failed to attend his meeting with the Soviet contact at the British Museum. May quickly confessed his espionage activities, explaining that he did so as a contribution to mankind (he had only received minimal payments from the Soviets).

He refused to provide any information about the spy ring, instead admitting that he had passed along information to the Russian, who were allies during the war, therefore shielding himself from a possible death sentence for collaborating with the enemy.

He pleaded guilty to treason on May 1, 1946 and was sentenced to ten years in prison at the Wakefield Prison in Yorkshire. He was released in 1953 after time off for good behaviour, and became a professor of physics at the University of Ghana and was later believed to have returned to be an employ of the Soviet Union.

Hans Oster

German Army General who Established a Resistance Organisation Against the Nazis

Born in 1888 in Dresden, Germany, Hans Oster was the son of a protestant parishioner.

He served as a General Staff officer in the German Army during World War I. He was a member of Reichswehr, the limited German Army allowed as part of the Versailles Treaty. He served in the German War Ministry beginning in 1933, later becoming a Colonel, where he headed the Second Department of the Abwehr (oversaw records of German intelligence agents).

A man of moral character, Oster felt disdain for the Nazi movement and contempt for Nazi Fuehrer Adolph Hitler. He aligned himself with other high-ranking officers who felt the same (including spymasters Wilhelm Canaris and Erwin von Lahousen). Clandestinely aided in the escape of Jews from Germany by funnelling money to them on the pretence of sending them out to spy in Switzerland.

Manfred Roeder of the Reich Military court launched an investigation into Army personnel working against the Nazi Party and discovered notes indicating Oster's involvement in helping the Jews escape as well as others which detailed attempts to negotiate a separate peace negotiation with the German Army and the Allies (brokered through the Vatican). Canaris was forced to dismiss Oster.

Oster continued his activities, attempting to oust Hitler. He participated in the ill-fated plot to explode a bomb on a plane in which Hitler would be a passenger as well as the attempt to detonate a bomb during a meeting (both attempts failed). As conspirators were rounded up, Oster was at the top of the list and was immediately arrested.

Oster was executed on April 9, 1945 at the Flossenburg concentration camp.

Ronald Pelton

American Spy Convicted of Passing NSA Secrets to the KGB

Born in 1942, Ronald Pelton attended Indiana University. He joined the U.S. Air Force and was assigned to the Signal Intelligence division in Pakistan. After leaving the Air Force, he joined the NSA in 1965. He worked in a minor capacity for the NSA until he resigned his position as an intelligence analyst in 1979.

He contacted the Soviet Embassy in Washington, DC on January 14, 1980 and explained to the diplomat that he was a member of the U.S. Government and arranged for a meeting at the embassy. The FBI had surveillance on the embassy and had tapped the phone. Although anticipated the arrival of the caller, the FBI was unable to observe him in time to determine his identity. The investigation seemingly died out there.

Pelton met with KGB officer Vitaly Yurchenko and provided him with detailed reports of U.S. activity from his photographic memory. Among the things he provided was a disclosure that the U.S. was monitoring underwater Soviet communications using submarines in the Sea of Okhotsk. Yurchenko accepted Pelton as a legitimate walk-in.

In 1985, Yurchenko defected to the United States. Among other things, he recalled that he had met with a former NSA analyst in 1980 and described him as red-haired (Yurchenko subsequently defected back to the Soviet Union). The FBI scoured through NSA personnel files until it had a pool of red-haired male analysts. They were thus able to identify Pelton's voice and began surveillance on him in October 1985. Despite bugging his car and his home, they were unable to turn up any incriminating evidence against Pelton.

Seemingly at a dead-end, the FBI decided to gamble and confront Pelton directly, playing the tape of his conversation with the Soviet embassy. Eventually, Pelton revealed that he had provided answers to questions from the Soviets in return for $35,000. Pelton was tried and convicted of espionage in 1986 and sentenced to three concurrent life sentences.

Oleg Penkovsky

Soviet Colonel who Exposed the Existence of Soviet Missiles in Cuba

Oleg Penkovsky was born in 1919 in Ordzhonikize, Russia. He was the son of a Czarist Army officer who fought against the Bolsheviks during the Russian Civil War.

He attended an artillery school and then entered the Red Army in 1939, seeing action one year later against Finland. He sent to Moscow where he acted as a political officer and then saw action against the Nazis in 1944 and 1945. He married the daughter of one of the Soviet Generals in 1945.

He returned to Moscow to attend the Frunze Military Academy, graduating in 1948, after which he was assigned to the GRU and sent to the Military-Diplomatic Academy for intelligence training. He learned English while attending Frunze, making him a valuable asset for intelligence work, but he was hindered by the fact that his father has served as an officer loyal to the czar.

He was sent to Ankara in 1955 where he served as a military attaché in the Soviet Embassy. He distinguished himself as a brilliant and very meticulous agent, spying on Turkish and U.S. military installations in Turkey. He was again slighted by a superior regarding his father and is believed to have exposed that superior to members of the Turkish intelligence community.

Penkovsky was placed in the Dzerzhinsky Military Academy in 1958 where he was trained in rocketry and missile weaponry. He was prepared to take on a new assignment in India but was once again slighted because of his father's past. Lingering frustration began to evolve into a serious disillusionment. He began to feel that the Soviet Union and Communism under Premier Nikita Khrushchev were mostly focused amass control of Europe and much of the world. He started considering making contact with Western agents shortly thereafter.

He was sent to London under the guise of heading up a trade delegation, but was actually supposed to setup and oversee a spy network. He had attempted to make contact with the West previously but had been unsuccessful. Before he left for London, he gave a package to Greville Wynne, a British businessman, who delivered it to the British Embassy in Moscow. Indicating that he wanted to provide information to the Western powers (Britain and the U.S), Penkovsky met a receptive audience. He was debriefed by a joint MI6-CIA contingent and Penkovsky warned that the Soviet Union would likely send missiles to Cuba. The level of detail that Penkovsky provided as well as the nature of his disclosures shocked the incredulous Western agents.

He was made a double agent, pretending to pass classified information to the Soviet Union while actually passing it to the U.S., and Britain and was given the codenames "hero" by the U.S. and "Yoga" by Britain.

While most information was gained during extensive debriefings (he would ultimately spend more than 140 hours being debriefed), Penkovsky also passed information to U.S. agents, including Wynne and Janet Chisholm, a former MI6 secretary and wife of a MI6 intelligence officer.

He provided vital information about Soviet plans for East Berlin and evidence that the United States had a clear advantage in the number and sophistication of missile weaponry.

KGB officials became aware that many of their secrets were being received by the West. After an investigation, their focus centered on Penkovsky. Although he was monitored, he was not immediately arrested. Finally, on October 22, 1962, Penkovsky was arrested by KGB agents. Wynne was arrested a few weeks later and was subsequently sentenced to three years in prison and five years in a labour camp. Penkovsky, on the other hand, was tried in a highly publicized media circus. He was convicted and sentenced to death, executed in May 1963.

Penkovsky was one of the most valuable double agents ever to work with the West. Because of his efforts, more than 300 KGB and GRU agents were recalled back to the Soviet Union and the head of the GRU, Ivan Serov, was fired and reportedly killed himself.

Kim Philby

High-ranking Member of British Intelligence who Worked as a Spy for the Soviet Union

Born Harold A. R. Philby in 1912 in Ambala, Punjab, India, became famous as Kim Philby.

His family was very well off, his father being St. John Philby, a famous explorer and adventurer who was assigned to India as an assistant commissioner for Punjab. The best man at St. John's wedding in 1910 was Bernard Montgomery who would ultimately become the most famous British general of World War II. Harold was given the nickname Kim by his father, after the spy hero of a Rudyard Kipling novel.

He graduated from Westminster before entering Trinity College at Cambridge in 1929 where he studied history. While in school he was recruited by Soviet intelligence, as were his friends Anthony Blunt, Guy Burgess and Donald Maclean. He worked as an NKVD agent, travelling on vacations to France, Austria, Germany and other areas of Europe that he thought were ready for revolution. He related his evaluation to his Soviet handler. While in Germany, he took part in open hostilities against Nazi Brown shirts, working alongside of the

Communists. He later helped set up a front organisation, the World Peace Congress. He graduated from Trinity in 1933.

He travelled to Vienna, Austria in 1934 and married Alice Friedman, also a communist. He was sent to Spain where he worked as a correspondent for the London General Press new agency, covering the Spanish Civil War. He worked under the guise of being a supporter of Generalissimo Francisco Franco and as well as being against the communist cause. He became associated with the ring wing Anglo-German Fellowship organisation, which was sympathetic to Nazi causes. As such, because of his pro-Fascist persona, he was welcomed into Franco party headquarters and followed Franco from city to city as he moved. Philby obtained information from Falangist officers and reported this back to his Soviet contacts. He left Spain in 1939 and separated from Friedman, in part to disassociate from her known pro-communist stance.

He was hired by the London Times to serve as a German correspondent. Because of his pro-Fascist persona, Philby was able to obtain information on the Nazis and passed it along to his Soviet contacts. He was invited to formal and private dinner with prominent Nazi officials and military figures, so his information was particularly valuable.

At the outbreak of war between Britain and Germany Philby was working with the British Expedentiary Force in France. British military officials recognised him as a noted war correspondent and were therefore comfortable with sharing information with him. Philby immediately passed this information on to Moscow.

After Germany defeated France, Philby returned to Britain. Despite his previous membership in the pro-Fascist Anglo-German Fellowship as well as his wife's communist past, Philby was brought into the British Secret Intelligence Service in 1941 (he was aided by his father, who contacted Sir Stewart Menzies, the head of SIS, directly. As part of the counterespionage division of SIS, he coordinated information exchanges between MI6 agents and Sandor Rado Soviet spy ring in Switzerland, obtaining valuable military information for Britain. He was also aligned closely with the Special Operations Executive, an espionage network which worked with underground resistance forces fighting against Germany. His success in these areas gained him high praise within the British intelligence community.

In October 1944, he was assigned to Section IX of SIS, establishing an anti-communist desk. He was in charge of a movement to seek out communists in the British government, particularly those who had infiltrated British intelligence agencies. The basis for placing Philby in this position was his familiarity and friendliness with high-ranking Russian military and diplomatic officials. Philby's new Soviet handler was Anatoli Lebedev. Philby grew the section from a one man shop to a 30 person department in only 18 months. He worked hand in hand with William J. Donovan and Allen Dulles of the United States Office of Strategic Services, the predecessor of the Central Intelligence Agency.

He barely escape exposure in August 1945 when Konstantin Volkov, vice consul at the Soviet consulate in Istanbul, defected. Volkov, an NKVD intelligence officer, warned of several moles in the British intelligence community, including one who was the head of a counterintelligence unit. Volkov warned against sending the information to Britain via cable because of security concerns.

The information was therefore delivered via diplomatic pouch and ended up on the desk of Kim Philby. An astonished Philby recognised that he was one of the moles Volkov was about to uncover. Philby insisted in interviewing Volkov himself, instead of leaving that task to an agent in Istanbul. By the time Philby arrived there, however, Volkov had disappeared, presumably executed after Philby notified to the Soviets about the impending defection.

When Igor Gouzinko, a Soviet cipher clerk in Ottawa, Canada defected in September 1945, Philby managed the information very well. Although a number of Soviet agents were exposed (including Allan Nunn May).

He was awarded the Order of the British Empire in late 1945 for his work in wartime intelligence work, after being nominated by Sir Stewart Menzies.

He divorced Alice Friedman and in 1946 married Aileen Furse with whom he had three children. He was sent during this period of time to Istanbul, Turkey, a hotbed for espionage activity in post-war Europe, serving as acting first Secretary of the Foreign Office. In this position, he identified to his Soviet handler, several Albanian nationalists planning to overthrow the communist government in place. The operatives were summarily captured and murdered. He also worked to foil British and American invasion of Albania, while at the same time passing along information about Soviet plans for the region. He was commended for his information which was ultimately useless due to its untimeliness.

He was sent to the United States in 1949 to serve as the First Secretary to the British Ambassador in Washington, D.C., acting as a liaison officer between British Intelligence and the CIA and FBI. This placed him in the position of working amongst the elite of the Western intelligence committee. Guy Burgess was also assigned to Washington, D.C. and they two worked together to channel information to Moscow. They met every week with James Angleton, sharing information and coordinating counterespionage efforts.

He received reports that Donald MacLean, another member of the Cambridge Five and alleged to have been Burgess' lover, was suspected of being a Soviet mole and warned the KGB of the matter. Learned that MacLean and Burgess might soon be arrested. Philby warned Burgess but also warned SIS that MacLean might be the person identified by Soviet defectors as being Soviet agent from a "good family" who served as a high-ranking Foreign Office official. Philby hoped that once MacLean escaped, any evidence that could point to him (Philby) would disappear also. In May 1951, Burgess and MacLean, defected, fleeing to Moscow.

He came under immediate suspicion from British authorities because of his friendship with Burgess and MacLean. Further damaged by a report given to the CIA by a defector, Ismail Akhmedov-Ege, which identified Philby as a Soviet mole. Philby flatly denied the allegations and was interrogated intensely. Stewart Menzies rose to his defense, but Philby angrily resigned his position with the Foreign Office. He was further supported by future British Prime Minister Harold MacMillan who deemed Philby an "upstanding citizen" and a "hero". Based on this type of support, Philby was brought back into SIS.

He worked in Beirut under the guise of a correspondent. His wife Aileen died in December 1957 and he married Eleanor Brewer (former wife of Sam Pope Brewer in 1959. He was clearly believed to be a Soviet spy after Soviet defector Anatoli Golytsin named him. He was confronted with the mounting evidence by friend Nicholas Elliott, a British agent then working in Beirut, Lebanon. Elliott offered immunity from prosecution if Philby cooperated and Philby filed a two page confession the next day and submitted to three days of oral confessions. Fearing a long prison sentence like that given to George Blake, Philby fled to the Soviet Union, by way of a Polish cargo ship bound for the Russian port of Odessa. He became a Soviet citizen on July 3, 1963.

He was awarded the Order of Lenin and worked at the KGB headquarters where he was given the title of General. He was joined by his wife and children in 1963 but began having an affair with Don MacLean's wife Melinda, prompting Eleanor to move to the United States. He was introduced to Rufina Ivanova by defector George Blake and married her in December 1971. He died on May 11, 1988 and was buried in Moscow with full military honours as a KGB General. He was honoured with depiction on a Soviet postage stamp in 1990.

❖❖❖

Jonathan Pollard

American Naval Intelligence Analyst who spied for Israel

Born in 1954, Jonathan Pollard was the son of a microbiologist teaching at Notre Dame University in South Bend, Indiana. He was raised with a deep love for Israel instilled within him, often vowed to migrate to Israel to live and to aid in fighting against the country's enemies.

He was educated at Stanford University, graduating with a degree in Political Science in 1976 and enrolled in the Fletcher School of Law and Diplomacy at Tufts University. While in school, Pollard often reveled in telling school mates of his adventures related to his father's work with the CIA. He often created stories such as this, and even went so far as to enter fabricated information in an application for employment with the U.S. Government. After failing to complete his pursuits in graduate school, Pollard took a job with the U.S. Navy Intelligence, working as a research specialist in 1979.

He observed what he considered considerable anti-semitism within the dealings between the United States and Israeli. Pollard believed that the United States often withheld information from its ally.

In 1984, he was assigned to serve as an analyst for the Naval Investigation Service, given special clearances and access to sensitive materials. He often shared some of this information with confidants and acquaintances.

He was introduced to Israeli war hero Colonel Aviem "Avi" Sella, who was serving as an Israeli operative under the cover of being a graduate student at New York University. At a meeting in May 1984, Pollard offered to supply Israel with sensitive information in order to help Israel in strengthening its defense systems. He turned over information related to Iraqi chemical weaponry. Another Israeli agent, Yosef Yagur, was assigned as Pollard's handler.

Pollard turned over thousands of documents to Yagur (he was able, because of his clearance, to simply check the documents out and take them home with him at night). In return, Pollard received $2,500 each month, as well as other gifts (including a diamond and sapphire engagement ring for his fiance, Anne Henderson).

Many of the secrets Pollard turned over were related to weaponry employed by Israel's enemies, including Iraq. Pollard gathered most of his information by searching Defense Intelligence Agency databases and conducted searches up to three times each week. Often, he provided original documents to his Israeli contacts, allowing them to photocopy them over the weekend, after which they would return them in time for him to return to work on Monday morning.

The range of materials that he provided included satellite photographs, weaponry assessments, and secret internal documents. Over time, Israel requested more and more information, and continued rewarding Pollard handsomely. He was treated to vacations in Europe (including his honeymoon) and was lavished with monetary gifts. At one point, he was presented with an Israeli passport and was told that a Swiss bank account had been opened on his behalf containing $30,000, along with a promise that $30,000 would be added for the next ten years.

Eventually, Pollard's excessive research and requests for data alerted officials at NIS, including his supervisor, Jerry Agee. An investigation found that several highly sensitive documents that he requested were not within his workspace, and thus likely had been removed from the building. The FBI was alerted and began observing him.

On November 18, 1985, Pollard was stopped and questioned by the FBI and NIS security officials. In his possession were several top secret documents. He was questioned repeatedly over the course of the next few days and growing desperate, ran to the Israeli embassy for safety. Followed by FBI surveillance teams, the Pollards were confident that they would find sanctuary within the gates of the embassy, but instead were denied. Demanding political asylum, he was ordered by Israeli security to leave the embassy grounds. The couple was soon thereafter arrested.

The fallout that Israel had engaged in espionage against the United States was immense. Public outcry and anger caused a backlash against Israel and jeopardised the country's political and intelligence relationship with the United States. Israel tried to deflect the blame for the activity, claiming it to be a rouge operation.

Pollard cooperated with U.S. officials, but argued that he was not spying against the United States, but rather for Israel, to whom he had a greater allegiance. He also argued that much of his information was basically useless to the Israelis but the prosecutors demonstrated that some of the material was funnelled by Soviet moles within the Israeli intelligence system and had compromised hundred of agents and friendlies in the Arab world.

Pollard pleaded guilty to espionage and was sentenced to life in prison. His wife was sentenced to two lesser crime and received a five year sentence, during which she complained vigorously about her treatment. She was released after three years and promptly divorced Pollard.

Pollard was considered a hero in Israel and many attempts were made to secure his release. Several Israeli officials made overtures towards the Bush and Clinton administrations but were denied.

Sandor Rado

Hungarian Cartographer who Spied on the Nazis for the Soviet Union

Born Alexander Radolfi in Budapest, Hungary, Sandor Rado, the son of a wealthy businessman, attended the University of Budapest, where he joined the Communist Party in 1919.

He took part in a revolutionary coup against the Hungarian government but the coup was put down quickly and Rado fled to Russia. He married fellow Communist Helene Jensen while in exile in Russia.

He was trained by the NKVD in 1931 and was assigned to a post in Berlin, Germany, working under the cover of a clerk in the Russian Embassy. He provided information on the strengthening position of the Nazi Party in Berlin and helped to organise demonstrations and violent uprisings against the Nazis by Communist Party members and a housewife, Howard Hansen who was part of a special division called the Red Unit, created to ferret out communist sympathisers during the Red Scare.

Fled to Paris, France to avoid capture (and probable execution) by Nazi hit squads (as a Jew and a Communist leader, he was specifically targeted). He created a publishing company called Geopress in Paris, which served as a cover for his Soviet spymaster activities.

He joined the GRI in 1936 and was posted in Switzerland, serving as Resident Director for Soviet intelligence within the country. Rado built a very successful network of spies named DORA. Members of his network included Ruth Kuczynski, Alexander Foote and Rachel Duebendorfer. Foote was actually a British agent, but he helped to feed information to Rado because the Soviet Union was an ally against Germany in World War II.

The DORA spy ring provided information to the Soviet Union about German military troop alignment. Some of this information was obtained from Rudolf Roessler, who ran the Lucy Spy Ring. Rado was not aware of his identity as Rado preferred to work through cut-outs. They provided detailed information regarding a German invasion of Russia. Despite having supporting information from another Soviet spy Richard Sorge, Soviet dictator Josef Stalin refused to believe that Hitler in fact planned such an invasion.

Rado was highly praised for the sophistication of his network and the level of reliability and detail of the information provided. Without the knowledge of Rado and the Soviet, much of the prized information was coming from the British, through Foote. The British had broken the Enigma code and therefore could read detailed German messages. Britain, however, did not want the Soviets to know they had broken enigma and thus passed information to Moscow through Foote.

Foote passed along additional detailed information proving that the German Army was going to launch another attack against Russia. The information was so detailed that Stalin relied on it this time and successfully defended itself from the Nazi onslaught.

Although he ran his spy network exceptionally well, Rado was known to drink too much and often made himself conspicuous through his lavish spending habits. Unknown to Rado, two of his agents were actually Nazi spies, passing along information to the German high command. Germany, therefore, threatened neutral Switzerland, demanding that the Swiss government arrest Rado and his entire spy network. Because the presence of the DORA spy ring had become so conspicuous, Switzerland felt it had no choice but to arrest members of the ring, lest Germany take military action.

After fleeing to France, Rado was ordered back to Moscow to explain how the DORA spy ring was shut down. Rado panicked, thinking he would be blamed for the failure and therefore put to death. Upon making a stopover in Cairo, Egypt, he fled from his companions and was found later hiding in a hotel room. He was immediately forced back to Moscow. Although he was believed to have been executed, Rado surfaced in 1955 in Budapest, where he was teaching cartography at Budapest University.

He died on August 20, 1981.

Alfred Redl

Austrian Head of Counterintelligence Blackmailed by Russia into Passing Secrets

Born in 1864, the son of a poor Austrian railroad official and one of 14 children, Alfred Redl rose to fame on his own.

He attended Lemberg Cadet School, a military academy and graduated in 1882. He received a commission in the Austrian Army. He was noted for his abilities with different languages. In 1889, he was assigned to serve as a military observer, accompanying the Russian Army. He made a number of friendship and contacts among the Russians.

He was continually promoted until he reached the rank of Colonel. At this point, he was placed in the Austrian Military Counterintelligence Corps. In 1900, he was named the head of the Kundschaftsstelle, the Austrian espionage and counterespionage service. He immediately set to work modernising the service, implementing new technologies as well as new methods for obtaining intelligence. Within his office, he often collected information on his visitors, obtaining their fingerprints by way of a special powder on the arms of their chair.

He also photographed and recorded the conversations of visitors to his office. He introduced a new method of interrogation, where he shined lights directly in a suspect's eye while questioning him – this he called the "third degree".

He was a homosexual, a fact that was kept a secret from any of his colleagues and superiors. He visited many of the most scandalous homosexual haunts throughout Europe. It is presumed that his homosexuality was discovered by the Russians and that they enticed him with young male lovers and then blackmailed him into providing information. At the same time, in addition to providing him with companions, they also paid him handsomely for providing them with secret information from the Austrian government.

Redl grew to possess lavish tastes and the funding from the Russians helped to afford him the lifestyle he desired. He revealed to the Russians identities of Austrian spies working in Russia as well as secret codes. In 1902, he provided the Russians with Austria's contingency plans in case of a war. The Austrian Foreign Office became aware that their contingency plans had fallen in the hands of the Russians, but had no idea who had delivered the plans. General Baron von Giesl turned the matter over to Redl, the Chief of Counterespionage. Redl was in the awkward position of having to conduct a search – for himself. He advised his Russian contacts of his dilemma and not wanting to lose such a valuable information resource, they gave a list of less important Austrians spying for Russia. Redl then "exposed" these agents, thus becoming a hero of the Austrian intelligence community.

He was promoted to head of all espionage efforts in Austria in 1907. In his position, conferred with intelligence officers from other nations, often discussing secret information with friendly allies, and then passing this information along to the Russians. He was promoted again in 1912 to the position of Chief of Staff to General von Giesl. Giesl headed up the Army Corps then in

Prague. Redl quickly passed along information about Giesl's troops to his Russian contacts. For his treachery, Redl was well rewarded. He used his ill gotten gains to purchase several houses in Vienna as well as a palatial estate outside the city. He purchased several of the most expensive cars in the world and a huge mansion in Prague, complete with an assembly of some of the finest champagne in the world.

On March 2, 1913, two letters, identically addressed were delivered to a postal box in Vienna. When nobody claimed them, they were returned to the post office in East Prussia from which they had been sent. The letters were sent back to Austria, this time to Redl's successor a Chief of Counterintelligence Maximilian Ronge. They were sent to him by the head of German counterintelligence Walther Nicholai who found them to contain large sums of money, with no letters accompanying them. Ronde recognised that the letters had originated from Eydtkuhnen, an area of East Prussia known for Russian espionage. Sensing that the money might be a payoff to a spy, he took the money back to the Vienna Post Office. He installed a button at the post office which rang through to the police station nearby. He instructed the postal clerks to push the buzzer if anyone came in to retrieve the letter.

After informing his superiors about what had occurred, Ronde, with a group of his men, entered Redl's hotel room and found Redl writing a note. Redl cordially welcome them in, telling them that he knew why they were there and that he was writing farewell letters. Asked the extent of his treachery, he referred Ronde to the Prague mansion, where he said all answers lay. Redl asked to borrow a revolver and five hours stood naked in front of a mirror surrounded by lights and shot himself in the head. Redl's last note stated "Levity and passion have destroyed me. Pray for me. I pay with my life for my sins. Alfred...".

The Austrian government attempted to keep quiet Redl deeds, but a hotel worker leaked information about the suicide, as did a locksmith brought in to help authorities break into Redl's house.

An examination of the Prague mansion revealed the level of income he was receiving from the Russians as well as the depth of his disloyalty. Thousand of secret documents were found as well as list of agents and contacts. Most significant was the discovery that information provided by Redl had been passed to Austria's biggest enemy, Serbia. Included in this was Austrian's plan in case of a war with Serbia. After a Serbian anarchist assassinated Archduke Franz Ferdinand, Austria did go to war against Serbia, but was repelled by the Serbian who knew their plans. Thus much of Europe and the United States was drawn into World War I.

Sidney Reilly

Russian-born British Spy Known for his Daring Exploits

Born Sigmund Georgievich Rosenblum in Odessa, Russia in 1874, Sidney Reilly was the son of a rich Jewish landowner. He was educated briefly through grade school but was largely self-taught from thereon. Over the years, he became proficient as a linguist, learning to speak at least seven languages fluently.

He left Russia at the age of 19, stowing away on a ship and travelling to Brazil. He worked in Brazil in various occupations, including as a dishwasher, a cook and a bouncer.

He served as part of an expedition through the jungle in Brazil, working as a cook for a group of British explorers. The group was attacked by cannibals and Reilly bravely grabbed a revolver and shot several of the attackers dead, driving off the rest. The grateful explorers invited Reilly to return with them to England. Impressed with his language skills, they steered him in the direction of the intelligence community.

He received training in espionage and was dispatched by the British back to Russia to gather information. Returning successfully, Reilly was given a permanent position with the British Naval Intelligence Department (NID).

He was very popular with the ladies, carrying on several affairs. He had a brief affair with noted author Ethel Voynick, later began an affair with Margaret Callahan, the young wife of Reverend Hugh Thomas. Reilly had met Reverend Thomas advising him on cures for his kidney. When Thomas was found dead in his room at the Newhaven Harbour Station hotel, a person claiming to be a doctor named T.W.Andrew, who bore a strong resemblance to Reilly, certified the death as a result of generic influenza and ordered no inquest be held. Despite the fact that there was no record of a doctor by that name in Great Britain at the time, Thomas' wife Margaret inherited about £800,000. Reilly subsequently married her on August 22, 1898. At this time, he discarded the name Sigmund Rosenblum and became known as Sidney George Reilly. He was granted British citizenship soon thereafter.

He was sent by NID to Holland during the Boer War where he was to gather information on the armaments shipments being sent to South Africa. He used his innate ability for disguise to assume identities and assumed the role of a Russian arms purchaser. Under this guise, he put himself in a position to inspect the arms development at certain Dutch facilities. Once again, he returned to Britain with valuable information. He impressed his superiors. He enjoyed similar success on a number of other assignments and became known within NID as one of the top agent within the agency.

He had a natural flair for his assignments, cool-headed, creative and brave. A master of disguise, he also possessed remarkable acting skills, allowing him to don almost any persona. He also possessed confidence and bravery that prompted him to accept even the most dangerous and impossible assignments.

He was allocated large blocks of cash to use to bribe officials and informants. He was also afforded a hefty salary, allowing him to enjoy a life of luxury outside his dangerous work and enjoyed the company of numerous women. It was said of him that he had as many wives as he had forged passports (which were numerous, indeed). He used his charm as a method for obtaining information from the wives of important officials.

While in the service of England, Reilly's true loyalty was to himself and his bank account. He would go to any extreme to accomplish the most dangerous mission so far as it would enhance his position, thereby prompting his superiors to call on him again. His willingness to risk life and limb was what made him so attractive as an agent to NID, it should also have alerted the agency to his willingness to do anything for money, a trait that would make him a prime target to be recruited by a rival intelligence service.

Upon return from Holland, he was assigned to Persia where vast oil deposits had recently been discovered. The Shah of Persia (now Iran) Mozaffar al-Din Shah Qajar had recently granted oil concessions to William Knox D'Arcy, an Australian businessman, allowing D'Arcy of most of the oil found in the country. D'Arcy was rumoured to be negotiating with France for the sale of rights to the oil and with England being among those in the running (along with Germany, France and Russia), Reilly sought to intervene. Disguised as a Catholic priest, Reilly barged into D'Arcy's office as he prepared for a meeting with the French. Reilly begged D'Arcy to give him a few minutes to discuss a charity he was involved with, but when D'Arcy took him to an adjoining room, Reilly admitted his real reason for being there. Incredibly, he quickly convinced D'Arcy to grant the concessions to England, thus setting into motion the creation of the Anglo-Persian Oil Company (later renamed the British Petroleum Co., Ltd).

He was sent to Port Arthur, Manchuria, a naval base for the Russian Far Eastern fleet. Accompanied by his wife, he was provided with an enormous bank account, the funds from which he purchased an interest in a small timber company as well as a Danish company (for whom he served as a manager). In reality, these were covers for his real business, spying on the Russian naval assets in Port Arthur. Reilly observed and recorded the positions and schedules of Russian warships as well as assessments of their armaments, crews and capabilities. He even drew sketches of the ships and the port. Reilly sent this information back to England, but was believed by some to have financial dealings with Russian and Japanese intelligence officers.

He was brought into the Secret intelligence Service (later known as MI6) in 1909 and served under Captain Mansfield Smith-Cumming. While SIS and NID were pleased with Reilly's capabilities and results, Smith-Cumming said of Reilly "He is a man of indomitable courage, a genius as an agent, but a sinister whom I could never bring myself wholly to trust".

He was sent to Essen, Germany in 1909 to monitor the vast growth of the German war machine. He devised a cover as a Baltic shipyard worker named Karl Khan secured a job as a welder in a Krupp armaments plant. His plan was to photograph the plant and its production output, but he realised that the drawing office was heavily guarded during the day. Instead, he volunteered for the fire brigade which worked during the night shift. A few nights later, he strangled the head of the night security detail and incapacitated another security officer, thereby gaining access to the drawing room. In truth, in place of bothering with photographing the plans, Reilty simply stole them, hopped a train and then a boat and evaded German agents as he escaped back to England.

With England still interested in Germany's naval and military capabilities, Reilly was sent to Russia where he posed as an armament distributor. Believing that aerial reconnaissance would provide the best opportunity for seeing and assessing the strength of the German fleet, he used his burgeoning bank account to sponsor air races for Russian aviators. In addition to establishing him as a member of the social elite, it also enabled him cover for flying over areas of the Baltic Sea, photographing German vessels. Through his newfound social connections, Reilly was introduced to a man named Massino, the assistant to the Russian Minister of Marine. Reilly seduced Massino's wife, Nadine, who confided that a German company, Blohm & Voss, were seeking to win the contracts to rebuild the Russian fleet. Reilly bought a small company (Mendrochovich & Lubersky) and pursuaded Massino to convince Blohm & Voss to name his company as their St. Petersburg agents. After Blohm & Voss was awarded the contracts to rebuild the Russian fleet, they sent copies of all of their designs to Reilly's firm, the designs having been based on the German fleet. Before he turned the plans over to the Russian Minister of Marine, he made a full set of photographic copies, which he sent back to England.

He was able to reach an agreement with SIS so that any profits he earned through his "cover" businesses were kept by him. Reilly became very wealthy through his SIS funded endeavours.

Enjoying Russia, he stayed, living a life of luxury and social prominence. He purchased a small palace where he entertained Nadine Massino and a bevy of other beautiful women. Eventually, he planted stories in Russian newspapers claiming his wife Margaret had died in a train crash. He then paid Massino a large sum of money to divorce Nadine, whom Reilly eventually married in New York City in 1916.

He was engaged by Russia to purchase arms for its war effort. Reilly purchased arms from the United States and from Japan.

He was assigned a new mission at the behest of British Prime Minister David Lloyd George. With the Russian government in tatters (after the overthrow of Czar Nicholas) Alexander Kerensky had taken control of the government as the new Prime Minister and was struggling to keep Russian in the fight of World War I. Ultimately, the Bolsheviks overthrew the Russian government and under the revolution's leader Vladimir Lenin, signed a peace treaty with the Germans in 1918. Reilly, in cooperation with Robert Bruce Lockhart, the British general counsel to Russia, attempted to overthrow the new Russian (Bolshevik) government in order to bring Russia back into the war.

He was assigned a new mission for England, and was sent to Germany again, this time to assess German army strength and movements. Speaking German fluently, he actually joined the German army and served on the Western front, while sending detailed assessments of German troop plans back to England via carrier pigeons.

He claimed to have impersonated the Chief of Staff to Rupert of Bavaria, thereby gaining access to planning conferences of the German high command. He collected information of great importance that he passed back to London.

He tried to deal directly with Lenin, turning up at the Kremlin gates, demanding to see the Russian leader (infuriating Lockhart in so doing).

He thought that the best way to overthrow the Russian government was to assassinate Lenin. He began to plot his assassination and bribed two of Lenin's bodyguards, who agreed to help him. He also began consolidating factions of anti-Bolsheviks to take part in the plot and compiled a list of Russian military leaders to take over after the fall of the Bolshevik government.

Before Reilly could act, Lenin was shot by a woman, Fanya "Dora" Kaplan. Lenin survived and after Kaplan was executed, the Bolsheviks began to search for a plot and tracked down the two guards Reilly had bribed. They cooperated and identified Reilly as well as Lockhart. Reilly eventually escaped on a Dutch freighter. Nonetheless, he was tried in absentia and was convicted of conspiracy against the Bolshevik government and against the life of Vladimir Lenin. He was sentenced to death.

Despite his failure, his flight and his death sentence, Reilly was convinced that he could have won Lenin and overthrow the Bolshevik government, begging Smith-Cumming to send him back in. The SIS chief declined. Nonplussed, Reilly endeavoured to carry out his own mission.

He formed an alliance with anti-Communist Boris Sakinov, the head of the counter-revolutionary Union for the Defense of the Fatherland and Freedom. Sakinov was able to gain a following of 30,000 anti-Bolshevik troops. Unfortunately anti-Bolshevik forces within Russia were soundly defeated before Sakinov could lead his troops into the country. Despite this, Sakinov was elated to find other pro-Monarchist anti-Bolsheviks in Paris who agreed to fund his counter-revolution. The Monarchist Union of Central Russia (also known as the Trust) sent him to Russia to meet with underground Trust sympathizers.

In truth, the Trust, a front group, created by the Bolsheviks under the guidance of Feliks Dzerzhinsky (OGPU). Months later, Reily was introduced to "Trust" members who led him to Russia to meet with the Trust's council leaders. Upon crossing the Finnish border, he was arrested on February 27, 1925 and taken to Lubyanka Prison where he was interrogated.

He was notified that the death sentence against him was to be carried out. Reilly, according to Soviet reports, tried to barter with Dzerzhinsky, promising to pass along British and American intelligence secrets in return for his life. It was to no avail.

He was executed by firing squad on November 5, 1925 outside of Moscow and buried in an unmarked grave.

Marthe Richer

A Former Prostitute who Spied for France Against Germany

Born Marthe Betenfeld in Blamont, France in 1889, Marthe Richer was the daughter of a brewer.

She was an excellent student, and excelled at languages, eventually learning to speak English, Spanish and German in addition to her native French. She was also adventurous, excelling as an aviator, almost unheard of for a woman at that time.

Married to Henri Richer, a pilot serving in World War I, in 1914, she was approached by French counterintelligence and was recruited for service based on her language skills as well as her daring personality. After her husband was killed in battle, Marthe distracted herself from her grief by travelling to Spain to undertake intelligence duties. She became a familiar face within the social elite of German society within Spain and was introduced to the acting chief of the Abwehr. He suggested to Richer that she should work as an agent of the Abwehr, returning to France and spying on behalf of the Germans. Richer told him that she would only consider doing so if the offer was extended by the head of the Abwehr in France himself. So eager were the Germans that they agreed and the offer was so extended. Fortuitously, the Abwehr chief in France was Baron Hans Kron. Kron, who was also the German naval attache in Madrid, fell in love with Richer and they became lovers soon thereafter.

Richer was shipped off to France to gain information on armaments production. She was provided with a new kind of security device, an invisible ink that was contained within a capsule, the size of a grain of rice. Upon arrival, she disclosed the invisible ink to her French superiors and informed them that she was involved with Kron. She was given doctored information about armaments production and was sent back to Spain.

In Spain, she re-established her relationship with her lover. She also learned that he had been involved with Mata Hari, the notorious spy who was staying in the same hotel as Richer. Threatening to break off her relationship with Kron, Richer was able to draw the love struck attache even deeper into her web, thus gaining access to even more secret information, which she passed back to the French, including revelations about submarine development.

Richer was sent across the globe on missions but eventually grew tired of the deception and the pressure. Eventually, she decided to return home to France but first confessed her duplicity to Baron Kron. After retiring from active service, Richer was generally ignored by the French government, based in part from unfavourable attention to her long-running relationship with the German attache. Eventually, her services were recognised and she was awarded the Legion of Honour medal in 1933.

She took part in the French resistance during World War II and died in 1982.

Rudolf Roessler

Head of a Soviet Espionage Ring that Spied on Germany

Born November 22, 1897 in Kaufbeuren, Bavaria, Rudolf Roessler was the son of a Bavarian forestry official and was educated in Augsburg.

During World War I, he served in the German Army. After the war, he began working as a journalist, serving for a time as a reporter in Augsburg and then as a literary critic in Berlin. He was friendly with members of the literary and artistic circles within Germany. Many of these friends were censored and targeted by the evolving Nazi power regime and were forced to flee the country for their lives.

Angry about the treatment of his friends as well as the emerging dictatorial regime in place, Roessler became a vehement opponent to the Nazi Party and to Adolph Hitler.

In 1933, he left Germany, moving with his wife to Lucerne, Switzerland where he established a small publishing company. With moderate success, the publishing company afforded him the funds to travel back and forth to Germany where he often met with prominent people within the literary, military and political arenas. An ardent German patriot, Roessler found that many of these associates felt exactly as he did and were just as concerned about the political and military changes in their country. A number of these associates pledged to share high level information to Roessler in the hope that he might be able to disseminate the information in a manner that would benefit. With friends in the German government and military, Roessler had privy to official secrets and military plans. He was able to know within 24 hours what the German Army planned to do and where.

Roessler insulated his sources from the Allied Forces, such that no one but he knew their true identities. One of his contacts, to whom he passed information, was Xavier Schneiper, a proponent of Marxism who despised the Nazis. Schneiper passed information obtained from Roessler to a Swiss underground intelligence operation known as Bureau Ha. In 1939, Roessler warned Schneiper of Hitler's intentions to invade Poland. He later provided Bureau Ha with explicit information detailing the Nazi's planned invasions of France, Belgium and Holland as well as Nazi intentions towards Switzerland.

He sent information through Sandor Rado's "Lucy" spy network (Lucy was Roessler's codename) providing specific times, dates and locations of a German invasion of Russia. This information was presented to Soviet intelligence but Josef Stalin refused to believe it and ignored it. Eventually, the Russians began to trust and rely on his information as it provided assessments of German troop strength and well as their plans for specific military activities. Many of these reports were delivered by Roessler mere hours after they were conceived and thus received by the Allies days, if not weeks before they were to be implemented. He further informed the Russians about what intelligence the Germans had about the Russian Army and its strategies.

Germany deduced that information was being passed to the Allies by persons located in neutral Switzerland. They complained to the Swiss. In an effort to placate the Nazis and therefore lessen the chances of a German invasion of

Switzerland, the Swiss government arrested a large number of the Lucy network spies, including Roessler in May 1944 (in doing so, the government may have, in effect, saved the lives of these spies rather than having the Nazis deal with them).

Roessler was tried by the Swiss government, but was found not guilty of espionage and released in September of 1944. Roessler actions in providing information to the Swiss likely contributed to his being found not guilty and he was allowed to return to his publishing company as the war was coming to a close.

Having financial difficulties in the post-War 1950's, Roessler was believed to have sold innocuous information about Allied occupation forces and he was again arrested for espionage. Found guilty, he was confined to prison for one year. He returned to his publishing company and lived out his life, impoverished, in Switzerland until his death in 1958.

Ethel Rosenberg

American Communist Executed for Espionage against the United States

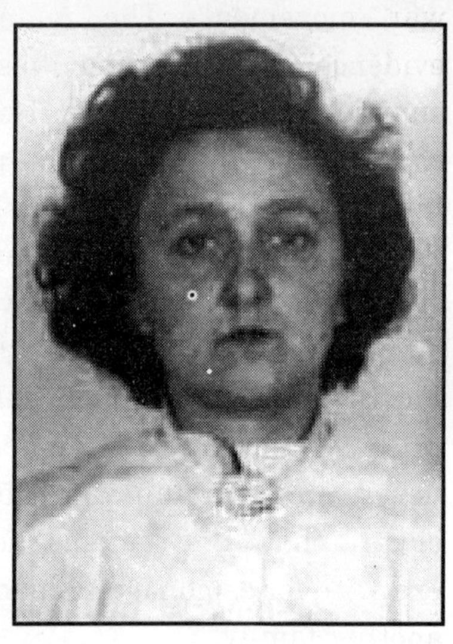

Ethel Greenglass Rosenberg was born in New York City on 25 September 1915. Her birth name was Ethel Greenglass. The family was very poor and lived in a shabby, unheated tenement. Ethel, the only daughter, attended Hebrew schools and Seward Park High School, graduating at age 15. She became a clerk for a shipping company, but was terminated for organising a women workers' strike to combat poor working conditions and low salaries. Ethel later joined the American Communist Party. At a New Years Eve benefit, she met Julius Rosenberg, who had been a civilian inspector for the Army Signal Corps during World War II. They married on June 18, 1939. Ethel became a homemaker for their sons, Michael and Robert. Julius opened a small machine shop in Manhattan with Ethel's brother, David Greenglass, but the business failed and Greenglass left the partnership. In 1950, Greenglass, who had been a low-ranking sergeant at Los Alamos Laboratory during the Manhattan Project, was arrested as a member of a spy ring that had supplied atomic secrets to the Russians. Greenglass claimed that Ethel and Julius were also members of the ring. They were arrested and tried under the Espionage Act, the 1917 law that had been passed to counter the American anti-war movement. The main evidence against them was supplied by Greenglass. He claimed that Julius had given him atomic bomb secrets, and that Ethel had typed David's notes. Despite the dearth of evidence against Ethel, she was found guilty of espionage with Julius, and on April 5, 1951 the couple was sentenced to death. For the next two years, Ethel lived on death row at Sing Sing prison, maintaining her innocence and hoping for leniency. It never came. On June 19, 1953, Ethel was put to death in the electric chair. She remains the only American woman ever to be executed for espionage. Her sons, aged 6 and 8, were adopted by another family.

Julius Rosenberg

American-born Soviet Recruiter and Atomic Spy

Born in 1918 in New York to Jewish immigrants from Russia. Groomed in the Orthodox Jewish faith to be a rabbi. He attended City College of New York with a degree in Electrical Engineering. While attending the school, he became a devout member of the Communist Party. He married Ethel Greenglass in 1939.

He began working for the United States Signal Corp in 1940 as a civilian employee. He was believed to have become a spy for the Soviet Union during this period of time, confiding his actions to his wife and seeking her aid with his activities. The Rosenbergs were believed to have been recruited by NKVD agent Gaik Ovakimian.

As he became more involved in espionage activities, Julius Rosenberg stepped back from his Communist Party activities so as not to draw attention to himself. He worked under the control of Soviet spymaster Anatoli Yakovlev, an attaché from the Russian Consulate in New York. Yakovlev instructed Julius to seek to obtain information related to the development of atomic weaponry, specifically the atomic bomb.

Ethel Rosenberg's brother David Greenglass was involved in the research taking place in Los Alamos, New Mexico on the atomic bomb. Codenamed "the Manhattan Project", the work involved many of the most respected scientific minds in the world. One of the people involved was Klaus Fuchs, a brilliant physicist from sent over from England.

Julius Rosenberg had begun working as an organiser and recruiter of spies and sought help from Greenglass. He convinced David's wife, Ruth Greenglass to visit him in New Mexico and obtain classified secrets about the atomic bomb from her husband, explaining that the information would be passed on to the Soviet Union so that the United States ally would be in a position to better defend itself against Nazi Germany. Ruth returned from her visit with names of scientists involved in the Manhattan Project, locations of test sites and descriptions of different experiments being conducted. She passed this information to the Rosenbergs.

In January 1945, while on leave from New Mexico, Greenglass met with Julius and Ethel. He had been a member of the Communist Party for several years already, persuaded to join by his sister Ethel. Emphasising the importance of his contributions, Julius took a box of Jell-O and tore it in half marking each half in a particular manner. He gave one half to David Greenglass and told him that a new Soviet contact would be arranged for him, recognisable because the contact would possess the other half of the box.

In June 1945, David was approached by Harry Gold, a Soviet agent who was also gathering information at the time from Klaus Fuchs. Gold showed Greenglass the other half of the Jell-O box as his identification. Greenglass gave Gold the documents that he had procured and Gold, in exchange, gave Greenglass $500.

In September 1945, Greenglass travelled to New York and met with the Rosenbergs. Here, he gave a detailed description of the Uranium bomb dropped on Hiroshima and the Plutonium bomb dropped on Nagasaki.

Although he was provided with an escape plan developed by the Soviets that would take him to Moscow by way of Mexico, David decided not to leave the United States. Subsequently, he was arrested on June 15, 1950. He quickly informed the FBI about the Julius Rosenberg and the spy ring that Julius was involved in. In spite of his preparations for the inevitability of arrest (Julius had obtained passport photos and applications for his family), Julius and Ethel did not flee in time (as had other Soviet spies, including Morris and Leona Cohen) and he was arrested on July 17, 1950. Ethel was subsequently arrested on August 11, 1950 and both were charged with espionage, as was Greenglass. Greenglass plead guilty while the Rosenbergs plead not guilty. Also arrested was Morton Sobell, another spy involved.

The Rosenbergs were tried in March of 1951 represented in the U.S. District Federal Court by the noted attorney Emanuel Bloch. Julius took the stand but denied involvement with anything actionable, repeatedly invoking his Fifth Amendment right against self-incrimination. Ethel did much the same. The jury found Ethel, Julius and Sobell guilty of espionage. Sobell was sentenced to 30 years in prison and Greenglass 15, but the judge harshly sentenced both of the Rosenbergs to death, a sentence aggressively sought by the Justice Department. The judge in the case, Irving Kaufman, reasoned that by passing the secrets to the Soviets, they had allowed the Soviet Union to begin building an atomic weapon years faster than it other would have, setting in motion a series of events that would ultimately lead to the Korean War.

The death sentences provoked world-wide criticism and charges of anti-Semitism, despite the fact that Judge Kaufman as well as two of the prosecutors was Jewish. It was believed that Ethel, whose role was much more limited than Julius' was sentenced to death in order to compel Julius to make a full confession, yet none would be forthcoming. More than 15 appeals to the United States Supreme Court and to President Harry Truman and Dwight Eisenhower were denied and the execution date was set for June 19, 1953.

Julius Rosenberg was executed in the electric chair at the Ossining Prison in upstate New York as was Ethel minutes later. Both maintained their innocence until the end. The Rosenberg case was hotly debated for years, with their innocence championed by their children. In 1995, however, the Venona messages were released, providing conclusive evidence that Julius was undoubtedly involved in espionage. Ethel, although unquestionably aware of Julius efforts, may not have participated sufficiently so as to justify a death sentence.

Agnes Smedley

American Journalist who Spied for Russia against Japan

Agnes Smedley was born in Missouri in 1892. She was eldest among children. Her father was a labourer and mother ran a boarding house. She moved to Colorado in 1902 and attended school.

She dropped out of grade school and didn't attend high school but enrolled in the Normal School in Tempe, Arizona. She married Ernest George Brundin on August 23, 1912 but divorced soon thereafter. She moved to New York City and attended lectures at New York University. She became involved in an Indian revolutionary movement (financed by Germany, then an enemy of Britain). She joined Friends of Freedom for India and assisted the group with hiding secret documents and information.

She moved to California in 1915, studying at the University of California but was arrested along with Salindranath Ghose, considered to be a political agitator. She was indicted for fraud (but not prosecuted). Then she moved to New York City but soon migrated to Berlin. She was aligned with Viren Chattopadhyaya who was also considered to be a Communist agitator. The two lived together for eight years.

She visited Moscow in 1921 for a meeting of Indian revolutionaries. After various illnesses, she began teaching English at the University of Berlin and founded a birth control clinic in Berlin before moving to Denmark. She wrote a book called "Daughter of the Earth" in 1927 continued her writings as a correspondent for the Frankfurther Zeiting. She was sent by Moscow to China in 1928, settling in Shanghai where she became an outspoken advocate of sexual freedom and women's issues as well as pushing other leftist issues.

She served as an agent for the Comintern and the GRV. She worked with Richard Sorge for a period of time and was believed to have been his lover. She had a vast network of useful contacts and introduced many of them to Sorge to use in his spy ring including Ozaki Hozumi and Ruth Kuczynski. She also introduced Sorge to radio operator Max Klaussen and continued as a war correspondent, chronicling activities in the Chinese revolution and served for a time in 1937 in the Eighth Route Army in the field.

During World War II she served as an advisor to Joseph Stillwell, the U.S. General and Military advisor to Chinese strongman Chiang Kai-Sheck, a noted anti-Communist. Persuaded Stillwell to arm Chinese Communist, convincing him that it was the lesser of two evils to help them fight against Japan.

She returned to the United States where she wrote and lectured about China and the Chinese people. She authored a book, "Battle Hymn of China", detailing her war experiences. She fell under FBI surveillance, and was labelled a Soviet agent after statements by Sorge were released which identified her as a Communist collaborator and a chief figure in his ability to conduct his operations. She was defended by several high ranking Washington politicians.

She threatened to sue U.S. General Douglas MacArthur libel for releasing Sorge's statements. MacArthur's chief intelligence officer Major General Charles Willoughby dared her to sue, claiming he had more than enough information to prove the allegations correct and threatened to publicly expose her. Smedley moved to England and was due to be called by the U.S. House American Activities Committee, but died of acute circulatory failure on 6th May, 1950 in a London nursing home and was buried in China.

❖❖❖

Richard Sorge

Soviet Master Spy who Ran a Spy Ring against Japan

Born October 4, 1895 in Baku, Russia, Richard Sorge was the son of Wilhelm Sorge, a German mining engineer and his Russian wife Nina. Wilhelm moved the family to Berlin, Germany in 1898.

He grew up very patriotic and nationalistic towards Germany, leaving school and enlisting in the German military in 1914. He served valiantly in the battle, and was wounded on three occasions. On the third occasion, he suffered severe injuries when shrapnel ripped through and broke both of his legs, the injuries causing him to endure a slight limp for the rest of his life. He was shipped back to Germany to recover. He started reading the teachings of Karl Marx, for whom his great Uncle had once worked. Disillusioned by the war and the nationalism that existed at the time in Germany, he left the military and focused on obtaining an education. Studying at several schools (including the University of Berlin, University of Kiev and University of Hamburg. He received a Ph.D. in Political Science in 1920. At about the same time, he joined the German Communist Party.

So profound was his belief in Communism that he began teaching it to his students while he was a teacher in Hamburg and then to fellow coal miners when he took a job in the mines a year later. He was terminated from both jobs. His actions were noted by the German police who labelled him as a Communist spy. As they prepared to arrest him, he slipped out of the country and headed to Moscow where he met Dimitri Manuilsky, the head of Intelligence for the Comintern. Manuilsky set in motion Sorge's training as a spy, encouraging him to learn English, French and Russian languages.

After significant training, Sorge returned to Germany where he married Christiane Gerlach in May 1921. While his wife was not aware of his espionage work, Sorge was taking more steps to establish himself in that field. He was ordered to move to Frankfurt where he would help to gather intelligence about members of the intellectual community as well as local officials. While in Frankfurt, he also worked to recruit new members into the Communist Party.

In 1923, Sorge met Russian scholar D. Riaznov who was looking to obtain original documents authored by Karl Marx. Sorge's uncle, Frederich Sorge, had previously served as Marx's personal secretary and Sorge was in possession of several of these documents. After providing these to Riaznov, Sorge was introduced by the scholar to a number of high ranking Russian intelligence officers.

Sorge and his wife soon travelled to Moscow where he met Communist Party officials and received his official Communist Party membership card. After being assigned to the OMS division of the Orgburo, Sorge undertook numerous intelligence operations. His wife, unhappy with the time consumed by his new duties divorced him.

He started working for the GRU in 1930, serving in the Fourth Bureau under General Yan Karlovich Berzin. Sorge was sent to Shanghai in 1930 to help in the attempt to initiate a Communist revolution in China. He gathered intelligence about Chinese leader Chiang Kai-shek and his supporters. Posed as an agricultural researcher, he was able to travel throughout China. He worked with underground Communist groups gathering information.

He was introduced to fellow agent Agnes Smedley in late 1930. Smedley put Sorge in contact with her boyfriend, news correspondent Hotsumi Ozaki, from whom Sorge would receive intelligence information for several years. Sorge also worked with a friend of Ozaki's named Teikichi, a correspondent, working for the Shanghai Weekly. He passed the information he gathered from these contacts and passed it on to another agent, radio operator Max Klausen. He was briefly involved with Soviet agent Ruth Kuczynski.

As hostilities between Japan and China escallated, Sorge reported back to Moscow about the readiness of Chinese troops and their chances against a superior Japanese military. After Ozaki returned to Japan in 1932, Sorge fell under suspicion of being a spy. He, therefore poured himself into his work as a journalist for almost a year. His writing appealed to members of Chang Kai-shek's military circle, who conferred with Sorge, thus unknowingly providing him with valuable information. He was identified as likely being an agent for Germany.

Sorge was recalled to Moscow in 1932 and met with great praise from his Soviet handlers. While in Russia he married a woman named Yekaterina Maximova. Soon thereafter, he was dispatched to Japan. Because of his excellent work product in China, his Soviet superiors felt that he might be the only agent that could obtain intelligence information in Japan which was at that time extremely secure against information leaks. He was assigned to determine whether Japan was prepared to move militarily against China, with a primary goal of determining the feasibility of developing a Soviet spy network in Japan.

Codenamed "Ramsey", Sorge went to Germany and obtained a German passport. Travelling as a German journalist, he arrived in Japan in September 1933. His spy cell was limited to himself and three other people in order to provide for maximum secrecy. He worked with Branko Vukelic, Yotoku Miyagi and a radio operator named Bernhardt. He immediately found that Benrhardt was a heavy drinker, a liability in that he was often too impaired to transmit his radio messages. In fact, at one point Sorge discovered that nearly half of his messages had not been transmitted by Bernhardt. Bernhardt was soon thereafter recalled to Moscow. Vukelic was quite adept at photographing documents obtained by Sorge and Sorge received information from Miyagi, courtesy of Sorge's old contact Ozaki.

The information that Sorge was receiving was extremely valuable to the Soviet intelligence officials to whom he reported. His information stream improved significantly in 1932 when Teikichi Kawai returned from China to Tokyo. Kawai began passing information he obtained from the Japanese Army personnel. As Sorge's information cache grew abundantly, he travelled back and forth from Japan and Russia to hand deliver it, since he did not have anyone to radio the information. Along his trip, he travelled through the United States where he met with Communist Party members and passed along their information.

Upon his visit to Moscow in 1935, Sorge met with General Uritsky, the head of the Fourth Bureau having replaced General Berzin when Josef Stalin came into power. Sorge showed detailed personnel charts of the Japanese military officers and their attitudes towards the Soviet Union, United States and Britain. Ozaki was officially brought back into the fold of his spy ring as was his former radio operator Max Klausen in November 1935. Sorge and Klausen met weekly for an information exchange while Klausen worked under the cover of a successful blueprints printer.

The Sorge spy ring came under the attention of Japanese intelligence and in January 1936 the Japanese secret police arrested Kawai, charging him with being a spy. Kawai, although interrogated and tortured over a period of six months in Manchuria, refused to provide any information and was subsequently released.

A military incident in February 1936 compelled the German Embassy to call Sorge in and give them an assessment of the political and military climate in Japan. So impressed were the Embassy officials that they considered Sorge a trusted ally and provided him with significant information about the Japanese government. Sorge quickly passed this information along to Moscow, including plans for an intended alliance between Germany and Japan. As his apparent value to the German government appeared to grow, so did his real value to the Soviet Union.

Sorge reported Japanese intentions to attack the United States and emphasised that Japan had no immediate intentions of engaging the Soviet Union in warfare.

The Sorge spy ring was compromised when Yotoku Miyagi was arrested by the police and interrogated over several days. Miyagi refused to talk despite repeated beatings by the police but attempted to commit suicide unsuccessfully by jumping out of a second floor window. He subsequently caved under pressure and acknowledged that he was a part of Sorge's Communist spy ring.

The Japanese High Police (Kempei Tai) were called in and arrested Ozaki, eventually beating a confession out of him. Although afraid of causing an International incident by arresting Sorge and Klausen, they decided to arrest them. On October 18, 1941, Japanese police conducted a sweep, arresting Sorge, Klausen and Vukelic. They discovered several messages in plain sight that Klausen was prepared to send to Moscow as well as evidence in the possession of Sorge and Vukelic. Klausen eventually implicated Sorge. Vukelic refused to admit anything. Vukelic would eventually draw life sentence as did Klausen. After six days of brutal torture, Sorge confessed to his part in the spy ring.

On November 7, 1944, Sorge and Ozaki were executed by hanging.

Sorge is remembered as one of the Soviet Union's most accomplished and valuable spies. He was named a hero of the Soviet state in 1964 and eventually had a postage stamp in his likeness issued.

Violette Szabo

French-born SOE Operative who Reconstituted a French Resistance Network

Violette Szabo was born in Paris in 1922 to a British taxi fleet owner and French mother, Violette Bushell. She was raised in Britain and married at a young age, but lost her husband when he was killed fighting against the Germans, leaving behind a young daughter.

Violette, a skilled shot with a rifle who could speak French fluently, was recruited into the SOE by Selwyn Jepson. A Raven-haired beauty, Szabo was considered a great candidate to work with the French underground. Her superiors, however, were greatly concerned with her urgent desire to put herself in danger, possibly a psychological reaction to her husband's death. They worried that she risked her life with a suicidal passion but they assigned her nonetheless.

Szabo flew through her training with merit and was placed with a former Havas news correspondent named Phillippe Liewer. She was dropped by parachute into France and was assigned to determine how many resistance forces were in place. She established communications between underground leaders and British intelligence forces. Making back to England, she was arrested twice by French gendarmes but was able to talk her way out of trouble and made her way to safety.

Upon reaching England, Szabo immediately sought another assignment, and although reluctant, her handlers sent her back into France. She passed along vital information to the French underground but was interrupted in one meeting when a German patrol discovered their meeting in a farmhouse. As one of the French resistance leaders fled, Szabo provided cover for him, shooting several German soldiers with a Sten gun. Eventually, her gun ran out and she was taken into custody.

Violette was taken to the Gestapo headquarters where she was raped repeatedly and tortured. Despite the cruelty, she refused to provide any information and was subsequently sent to Ravensbruck concentration camp. Upon reaching the camp, she was subjected to more brutal torture but again refused to talk to her captors, thus establishing her reputation for courage and bravery. After growing frustrated with her refusals, the Gestapo executed Violette in April 1945. In January 1947, she was posthumously awarded the George Cross by the British government acknowledging her valour.

Franz Von Papen

German Spymaster Assigned to Disrupt U.S. British Communication

Born in 1879 in Westphalia, Germany, Franz Von Papen the son of a member of the wealthy Junker class.

He was sent to New York City in 1915 where he worked at the German Consulate. He was assigned to act as a spymaster, overseeing agents assigned to disrupt the conveyance of military supplies from American manufacturers to Britain (the United States was a neutral party at the time while Britain was at war with Germany).

Under his direction, agents set up phony American armaments firms and contracted with Allied countries to provide them with arms. With the Allies hopelessly waiting, the agents would make excuses for continuous delays, with the arms never being delivered. Other schemes, he set into place had firms buying up gunpowder in huge quantities which preventing it from becoming available for the Allies.

After being saddled with a number of incompetent and reckless agents, Papen was directed to oversee numerous sabotage efforts against U.S. interests. He steadfastly refused, but did set up a scheme to blow up part of the Canadian Pacific Railway in order to thwart the efforts of Canadian troops to reach England to fight on behalf of the British. The scheme failed and the saboteurs were captured.

Papen also attempted to recruit German nationals living in the United States and persuading them to return to Germany to fight on behalf of their mother country. When this came to the attention of U.S. authorities, Papen was ordered to leave the United States.

He was assigned for a period of time to serve as a military attache in Spain where he came into contact with Mata Hari. He was later sent to Palestine where he was to aid the Turks in their war against England and especially in tracking down and crushing the insurgent troops under the leadership of T.H. Lawrence. These attempts were unsuccessful.

He became politically active after his return to Germany and eventually rose to the position of German chancellor. In 1939, after the ascension of Adolph Hitler, Papen was appointed the German Ambassador to Turkey. He once again acted as a spymaster in that country, competing against Allied spymasters for information.

In 1943, he was introduced to Elyeza Bazna, an Albanian working as a valet for the British Ambassador in Ankara. Bazna offered to provide Papen with secret British documents and information in return for money. Papen approved and Bazna was given the codename “Cicero”. Bazna’s information was invaluable, highly detailed and accurate, even covering meetings between U.S. President Franklin Roosevelt and British Prime Minister Winston Churchill and Allied plans for the invasion of Europe.

Bazna was compromised as Fritz Kopke, a German national working as an American agent, came across his name in a message from Papen to German Foreign Minister Joachim von

Ribbentrop and passed it on to Allen Dulles who thereafter passed it on to British Intelligence head Claude Dansey.

After the war, Papen was arrested and tried for war crimes at the Nuremberg Tribunal. It was found that his actions were not deemed to have reached a level sufficient to rise to "conspiracy to commit crimes against peace" as he was charged. He was thus found not guilty by the Nuremberg Tribunal. He was, however, arrested by the new German government and charged with various crimes committed during the Nazi regime. He was found guilty and sentenced to eight years in prison. Upon release, he wrote an autobiography documenting his activities. Papen died in 1979.

John Walker, Jr.

U.S. Military Communications Specialist who Created a Spy Ring to Pass Intelligence to the Soviets

John Walker, Jr. was born in July 28, 1937. He was the son of studio salesman for Warner Brothers. His father was a drunkard who cruelly beat his wife and children. John's hatred for his father prompted him to spend a week plotting his murder (he decided against it). Eventually, his father abandoned the family.

In 1955, John Walker was arrested for burglarising a gas station. Having confessed to several other crimes, a judge took the advice of John's older brother and allowed him to join the Navy rather than serve jail time. John's brother Arthur was a Naval and believed the discipline would be beneficial to his younger brother. John felt immediately that he was smarter than others with whom he served.

John Walker was stationed in Boston, Massachusetts and met a young woman named Barbara Crowley. The two began dating and when Barbara became pregnant they married. Barbara gave birth to a daughter (Margaret) and the family moved to Norfolk, Virginia after John was transferred to serve on a submarine as a radioman.

Barbara gave birth to two more girls (Cynthia and Laura) and a boy (Michael). Although, he was fairly successful in his job, the family saved all of their money in hopes of John opening a business. In 1966, he bought a house in Charleston, South Carolina which he turned into a bar (financed by his savings as well as a loan from Arthur).

The bar was largely a failure and the pressure contributed erratic behaviour from John. He began engaging in adulterous affairs and constant arguments with his wife. Barbara, likewise unhappy, turned to a surprising lover, John's older brother Arthur.

When John was transferred to Norfolk Virginia, he left Barbara and his family behind to look after the bar. In his new assignment, he served as watch officer in the radio room of the Atlantic Fleet headquarters. In his position, he obtained information on every U.S. submarine in the Atlantic Ocean. Despondent over monetary issues as well as his crumbling marriage, John decided to seek money out for the classified information he was privy to.

In 1967, John stole a key list, a document with codes used to encrypt and decipher classified messages. He took a copy of it and marched into the Soviet embassy in Washington, D.C. He explained to a KGB officer that he was interested in turning over military secrets in return for monthly payments from the Soviets. After looking over the document, the KGB officer agreed. Ignoring instructions from his Soviet handlers, Walker began spending money freely, raising the suspicions of his wife. She pried open a metal lock box in John's office in which she found photographic materials as well as maps and instructions for dead drops. She confronted John and he admitted that he was a spy. Barbara accompanied him to one of his dead drops (later claiming that she wanted to show support for him and their marriage).

John passed on information related to nuclear submarine classifications to the Soviet until he was transferred to San Diego, California to teach radio operations. Worried about losing access to vital information, he looked to develop another source. He found this source in Jerry Whitworth, one of his students. Walker wanted to retire from the Navy so that Barbara, angered over their marriage, would not be able to inform on him. Whitworth, newly assigned to Naval satellite communications school, readily agreed to participate.

Upon returning to Norfolk, John retired from the Navy and divorced Barbara. She and the children moved to Maine while he opened a private detective agency. His scheme with Whitworth ran smoothly until Whitworth began asking for more money and threatening to quit. Walker attempted to obtain more money from the Soviets but also decided to try to find more resources. He began with his children, approaching Margaret and Cynthia, both of whom rejected his advance. Although his daughter Laura entered the U.S. Army at his urging, she left the service after becoming pregnant. The KGB agreed to give Whitworth a pay raise, allowing his operations with Walker to control.

In 1979, Walker approached his brother Arthur, a retired Naval lieutenant commander about joining his spy ring. Arthur was now worker for a private defense contractor and began smuggling documents to John.

Not content with just two resources, John focused his attention on his son Michael. After getting involved with petty crimes in Maine, Michael was sent to live with his father. John befriended his son, getting women for him and engaging in smoking marijuana with him. John urged his son to use moderation with drugs and with other vices and also hired him to work with him on weekends with his detective agency. He began guiding him towards seeking a position in the Navy and Michael enlisted upon graduation from high school.

After being assigned to a ship, Michael was surprised when his father approached him to join his spy ring. Michael accepted and after being stationed aboard the U.S.S. Nimitz, he was assigned to dispose of top secret messages by burning them in a furnace. Instead, he rifled through the large bags of documents, taking those of interest out and destroying the rest. He also uncovered the codes needed to open safes containing more top secret information, which he passed on as well.

In 1984, Barbara Walker discovered that John seemed to have an unlimited source of money but had refused to provide her with alimony payments. She threatened to expose his spy ring, not knowing that her son Michael was involved in it. He and Michael discussed informing her of Michael's involvement so as to head off possible exposure but both neglected to do so. On November 17, 1984, Barbara contacted the Boston office of the FBI, informing them that her former husband was a spy.

Barbara was initially considered a vindictive ex-wife but a report of the discussion landed on the desk of Norfolk based FBI agents Joseph Wolfinger and Robert Hunter. After she passed a polygraph test and provided specific details about dead drops, she also told them that John had tried to recruit her daughter Laura. Hunter was dispatched to Buffalo, New York where he interviewed Laura. She corroborated Barbara's story leading the FBI to place a wiretap on John's telephone. Evidence gathered from this wiretap prompted agents to set into an action plan to catch him in the act of passing classified documents.

After dispatching cars and a small aircraft to tail Walker, surveillance lost him as he cased his dead drop location. Barbara had told the FBI that John often did a practice run beforehand, so agents waited, hoping that he would return and make a drop. After making the drop, he drove to another location to pick up his payment but when he was unable to find one he went back to his drop where he found the information missing. Worried, he returned to his hotel to think.

At 3:30 a.m., Walker's telephone rang. The front desk clerk told Walker that the van had been struck by a car and suggested that he come to the front desk. A suspicious Walker suspected a plot but decided to check things out any way. Brandishing a gun, he checked the hallway and then went back to his room to grab incriminating evidence which he sought to hide. As soon as he exited his room, two FBI agents burst from an adjoining room with guns drawn and placed him under arrest. The information in his possession when he was arrested contained documents discussing all of the members of his spy ring. As the FBI found more and more evidence against the ring, John decided to cooperate by testifying against Jerry Whitworth and detailing the extent and reach of the ring in an attempt to gain a lenient sentence for his son Michael.

John Walker, Jerry Whitworth and Arthur Walker all received life sentences for their roles in the spy ring. Michael Walker received a 25 year sentence but was released on parole in 2000 after serving 15 years. Walker's spy ring was considered one of the most damaging ever in United States history. The extent of damage has been difficult to assess but the U.S. government has had to spend more than $1 billion changing codes and equipment compromised by Walker's activities.

Herbert Yardley

American Cryptologist who Wrote the Expose "The American Black Chamber"

Herbert Yardley was born in April 1889 in Worthington, Indiana. He learned about telegraphy from his father. He wanted to pursue a career as a lawyer but took a job after high school as a railway telegrapher.

In 1912, he took another job with the State Department as a telegraph operator. He seemed fascinated with codes and often decoded messages for President Woodrow Wilson. He argued that the President's coded messages were easy to break and that the coding mechanism was hopelessly outdated. He wrote a 100 page report which contained his conclusions. The title was exposition on the Solution of American Diplomatic Codes.

He was moved to the U.S. War Department in 1917 as the United States had entered World War I. He was given the rank of lieutenant and assigned to the U.S. Signal Corps where he was named head of the MI8 (Military Intelligence, Section), a section devoted to cryptology. He was assigned the task of cracking the German diplomatic codes and was successful, leading to the prosecution of German saboteurs, including Lothar Witzke.

He travelled to Europe and met with MI5 chief Vernon Kell and the chief of British Naval intelligence Admiral William Reginald Hall. He also met French cryptologists to compare tactics.

At the end of World War I, Yardley's section was designated to be disbanded. Yardley and General Marlborough Churchill, the head of Army Intelligence, insisted that the section was essential to diplomatic relations during peacetime. In order to diffuse attention on the group, the operation was moved to New York City, where they operated out of a brownstone.

The group was able to break the codes of the Cheka, the Russian secret police but was most renowned for the breaking of the Japanese diplomatic codes. The United States was embroiled in negotiations with Japan at the 1921 Washington Naval Conference, determining the allowable tonnage for naval warship for major military powers. The United States argued that the ratio should be 10:6 in favour of the U.S. over Japan. Japan insisted on a minimum of 10:7, but Yardley's group broke diplomatic codes allowing the U.S. to learn that the Japanese would accept 10:6 as a final compromise. The U.S. stood firm and the Japanese eventually agreed to the10:6 ratio.

In 1924, U.S. President Calvin Coolidge ordered a sharp cutback on federal spending and five years later, Henry Stimson, President Herbert Hoover's Secretary of State, deemed Yardley's section as non-essential. Stimson, highly offended at how diplomatic messages were being intercepted, reportedly declared "Gentlemen do not read each other's mail", and ordered State Department funding of Yardley's group to cease immediately. Yardley's group, officially called the Cipher Bureau but also known as the American Black Chamber, was thus shut down.

Ousted from the intelligence community, Yardley grew frustrated and angry at U.S. naivety as well as his shabby treatment. In 1931, he published a book called 'The American Black Chamber'. The book detailed his experiences in breaking codes and gave detailed explanations of the breaking of the Japanese codes. The book was serialised in the Saturday Evening Post, gaining fame and wealth for Yardley. It also caused him to fall into further disfavour with the U.S. Government and members of the intelligence community. In reaction to his book, Congress passed a bill prohibiting the publication of government secrets, including diplomatic codes and the bill was signed into law by President Franklin Roosevelt in 1933.

Yardley tried at several other ventures, including selling invisible ink to government agencies but once again returned to writing, authoring a manuscript called 'Japanese Diplomatic Secrets', but the book was seized by federal authorities before it reached the printing press. He next wrote of espionage-oriented comedy called 'The Blonde Countess' which was later made into a popular movie starring William Powell and Rosalind Russell. He also penned another novel called 'The Red Sun of Nippon'.

Although still ostracised in the U.S. intelligence community, he was welcomed in other countries. He travelled to China where he worked with Morris "Two-Gun" Cohen. Helping to coordinate intelligence matters under Chiang Kai-shek in China's was against Japan. He also was recruited by Canadian authorities to help them establish a code-breaking operation for the Canadian government.

After the United States entered World War II, Yardley returned to the United States where he obtained a job with the federal government but was kept out of cryptology matters and instead assigned to the Office of Price Administration.

After the end of World War II, Yardley, an avid poker player, wrote a book called "The Education of a Poker Player". He died a year later. He is known as the father of modern cryptology.

Abbreviations Explained

FBI FBI is a bureau of the U.S. Department of Justice that deals with matters of national security, interstate crime, and crimes against the government. It is full form Federal Bureau of Investigation.

NKVD NKVD is the Soviet secret police from 1934 to 1946. Its full form Narodny Kommissariat Vnutrennikh Del.

CIA CIA is U.S. federal bureau responsible for intelligence and counterintelligence activities outside the United States. In conjunction with the FBI, it is also involved in domestic counterintelligence. Its full form is Central Intelligence Agency.

OSS Office of Strategic Services.

GPU GPU is the Soviet secret police, from 1922 to 1923. Its full form is Gosudarstvennoe politicheskoe upravlenie.

MVD The Ministry for Internal Affairs in the former Soviet Union from 1946 to 1960, acting as secret police. Its full form is Ministerstvo vnutrennikh del.

MI5 M15 is a former official and current popular name for Military Intelligence, section five, the British security and counterintelligence service.

MI6 M16 is a former official and current popular name for Military Intelligence, section six, the British secret intelligence and espionage service.

ACP ACP is a group of over forty nonaligned developing countries with aid-related and economic links. Its full form is African, Caribbean and Pacific (countries).

NATO NATO or Nato an international organisation established in 1949 to promote mutual defense and collective security that was the primary Western alliance during the Cold War. Its full form is North Atlantic Treaty Organisation.

NSA National Security Agency.

PERSONALITY DEVELOPMENT

Available in Tamil also.

9450 B • Rs. 195/- 5642 A • Rs. 150/- 9447 C • Rs. 88/- 8966 E • Rs. 88/- 9973 E • Rs. 110/- 5639 B • Rs. 75/- 9070 B • Rs. 175/-

8868 D • Rs. 150/- 9028 D • Rs. 120/- 9981 B • Rs. 120/- 9088 C • Rs. 195/- 8997 B • Rs. 96/- 9430 B • Rs.150/-

STUDENT DEVELOPMENT

9457 E • Rs. 150/- 9455 C • Rs. 150/- 8962 A • Rs. 96/- 4016 D • Rs. 96/- 9089 D • Rs. 135/- 9967 C • Rs. 120/-

9071 D • Rs. 96/- 2244 D • Rs. 60/- Ⓗ 9441 S • Rs. 195/- 5622 A • Rs. 108/- 9090 A • Rs. 160/- 2241 J • Rs. 68/-

BODY/BEAUTY CARE

8093 D • Rs. 150/- 9986 B • Rs. 120/- 9922 F • Rs. 96/- 8865 F • Rs. 90/- 8971 B • Rs. 96/-

LOVE, SEX & ROMANCE

8260 D • Rs. 96/- 8266 D • Rs. 80/- 8278 C • Rs. 80/- 8916 D • Rs. 68/- 8268 C • Rs. 175/-

COMPUTERS

0000 • Rs. 150/- 7766 A • Rs. 120/- 9460 J • Rs. 12(

7712 K • Rs. 96/- 7711 J • Rs. 96/-

PARENTING

8261 D • Rs. 150/- 8919 D • Rs. 96/-

SAYINGS/QUOTATIONS/ PROVERBS

8963 B • Rs. 80/- 9953 A • Rs. 68/-

8999 D • Rs. 80/- 5512 A • Rs. 120

9346 C • Rs. 60/- 9425 A • Rs. 60/-

SELF-IMPROVEMENT

9449 A • Rs. 195/-

9096 B • Rs. 96/-

4008 J • Rs. 96/- Ⓑ

9027 D • Rs. 120-

8258 D • Rs. 120/-

9026 D • Rs. 175/-

9563 N • Rs. 125/-

8928 D • Rs. 80/-

9066 B • Rs. 96/-

9081 D • Rs. 96/-

4010 L • Rs. 60/-

9091 B • Rs. 80/-

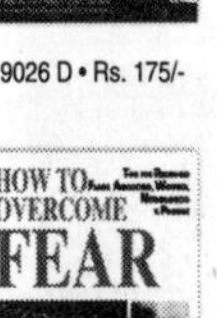

8885 D • Rs. 68/-

8947 E • Rs. 80/-

4009 K • Rs. 96/-

8943 C • Rs. 195/-

8935 D • Rs. 96/-

8990 C • Rs. 96/-

DIET & NUTRITION

9941 D • Rs. 96/-

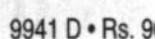

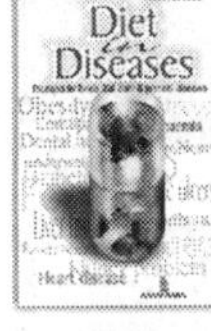

8985 B • Rs. 69/-

8904 D • Rs. 96/-

8276 A • Rs. 80/-

8968 G • Rs. 96/-

RELATIONSHIP

9458 G • Rs. 72/-

8998 C • Rs. 80/-

9438 B • Rs.150/-

9065 A • Rs. 80/-

9994 E • Rs. 120/-

JOB / CAREER

5623 B • Rs. 195/-

9404 D • Rs. 195/-

9439 C • Rs. 150/-

9431 C • Rs.175/-

4017 D • Rs. 120/-

4018 D • Rs. 80/-

9535 C • Rs. 150/-

ALTERNATIVE THERAPIES

8983 E • Rs. 80/-

8941 A • Rs. 80/-

8879 C • Rs. 60/-

5637 D • Rs. 96/-

8882 F • Rs. 150/-

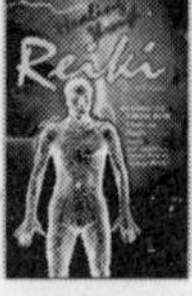

8842 D • Rs. 80/-

8889 D • Rs. 80/-

8836 D • Rs. 135/-

8271 C • Rs. 96/-

2317 E • Rs. 60/-

9935 F • Rs. 108/-

9950 B • Rs. 80/-

GENERAL HEALTH

8877 A • Rs. 120/-

8870 D • Rs. 60/-

9029 D • Rs. 68/-

9075 C • Rs. 160/-

9940 D • Rs. 120/-

8938 D • Rs. 88/-

8948 A • Rs. 96/-

9025 D • Rs. 80/-

9038 D • Rs. 68/-

8859 G • Rs. 80/-

SLIMMING & FITNESS

9445 A • Rs. 150/-

8277 B • Rs. 80/-

8875 K • Rs. 80/-

8847 M • Rs. 60/-

COMMON AILMENTS & DISEASES

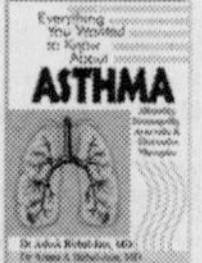

8281 A • Rs. 80/-

8094 D • Rs. 120/-

8888 D • Rs. 80/-

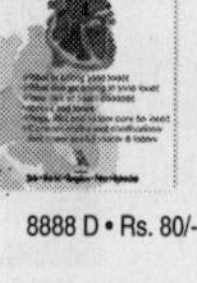

8908 D • Rs. 120/-

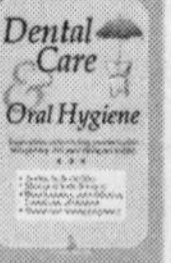

8964 C • Rs. 96/-

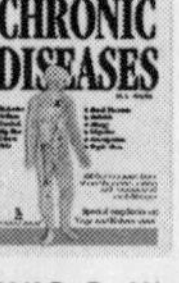

8848 D • Rs. 96/-

8878 B • Rs. 80/-

8891 D • Rs. 120/-

YOGA & MEDITATION

2118 F • Rs.120/-

8269 A • Rs.150/-

9087 B • Rs.96/-

9998 D • Rs.120/-

9080 C • Rs.24/-

8939 D • Rs.88/-

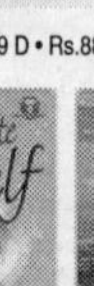

8099 D • Rs.80/-

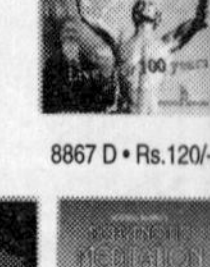

8867 D • Rs.120/-

8901 D • Rs.120/-

9958 S • Rs.160/- (with CD)

2119 G • Rs.96/-

8892 D • Rs.120/-

9057 B • Rs. 96/-

HOMEOPATHY

9446 B • Rs.150/-

8887 D • Rs.175/-

8270 B • Rs.165/-

HINDOOLOGY / RELIGION

9453 A • Rs.340/- HB
4128 D • Rs. 250/- Colour (H.B.)
4177 C • Rs. 295/- (H.B.)
9987 E • Rs. 150/-
9585 A • Rs. 96/-
9983 D • Rs. 499/- Colour (H.B.)

9508 D • Rs.95/-
4126 B • Rs. 96/-
9505 A • Rs.195/-
4183 A • Rs. 350/- (H.B.)
9514 B • Rs.60/-
4151 A • Rs. 399/- Colour (H.B.)

4133 A • Rs. 60/-
8898 D • Rs. 80/-
4124 A • Rs. 80/-
9405 A • Rs. 195/-
4190 C • Rs. 160/-
9984 E • Rs. 399/- Colour (H.B.)

9513 A • Rs.175/-
9520 D • Rs. 120/-
9510 B • Rs.120/-
9542 B • Rs. 150/-
4182 D • Rs. 96/-
4130 B • Rs. 120/-
4152 B • Rs. 96/-

4134 B • Rs. 80/-
9509 A • Rs.150/-
9407 C • Rs. 195/-
9525 A • Rs. 150/-
9504 D • Rs.96/-
9989 D • Rs. 96/-
4181 C • Rs. 195/-
9540 D • Rs. 150/-

9069 A • Rs. 80/-
4179 A • Rs. 295/- (H.B.)
4132 D • Rs. 80/-
9063 D • Rs. 80/-
9997 C • Rs. 80/-
9959 D • Rs. 80/-
4113 D • Rs. 48/-
4188 A • Rs. 160/-

COOKERY BOOKS

9936 D • Rs. 96/- 9320 A • Rs. 125/- 9297 C • Rs. 125/- 9948 D • Rs. 80/- 9938 D • Rs. 80/-

9962 C • Rs. 125/- 9942 D • Rs. 80/- 9944 D • Rs. 80/- 9943 D • Rs. 80/-

MYSTERIES / GHOSTS / ADVENTURE

2331 C • Rs. 60/- 2335 A • Rs. 80/- 9985 A • Rs. 80/- 5164 E • Rs. 72/-

9977 B • Rs. 96/- 2337 C • Rs. 96/- 2336 B • Rs. 80/- 51107 • Rs. 72/-

5156 D • Rs. 72/- 5172 F • Rs. 72/- 5121 K • Rs. 72/- 5116 D • Rs. 72/-

HOMEMAKING / GRILLS & RAILINGS

3111 E • Rs. 175/- 3107 F • Rs. 88/- 3106 E • Rs. 88/- 3108 G • Rs. 90/-

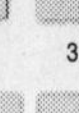

3102 K • Rs. 195/- (H.B.) 3103 L • Rs. 88/- 3104 M • Rs. 88/- 3105 D • Rs. 88/-

JOKES

2319 B • Rs. 96/- 2341 B • Rs. 60/- 2318 A • Rs. 80/- 2330 B • Rs. 80/- 9226 A • Rs. 60

HUMOUR & SATIRE

2338 D • Rs. 120/- 8890 D • Rs. 68/- 2315 C • Rs. 80/- 2321 D • Rs. 295/- (H.B.) 9340 A • Rs. 96/- 8927 D • Rs. 68/- 2326 E • Rs. 120/-

QUIZ BOOKS

8965 D • Rs. 96/- 7727 L • Rs. 72/- 7723 F • Rs. 72/- 7726 K • Rs. 72/- 7753 G • Rs. 72/- 7722 E • Rs. 72/- 7725 J • Rs. 72/-

Moral, Wisdom & Fairy Tales

8967 F • Rs. 96/- 9077 E • Rs. 120/-

9248 C • Rs. 60/- 2289 D • Rs. 72/-